KNITTING PLUS

KNITTING PLUS

Montse Stanley

B.T. Batsford Ltd, London

ISBN 0 7134 6004 0

Typeset by Servis Filmsetting Ltd, Manchester
and printed in Spain
by Graficas Estella SA
for the publishers
B. T. Batsford Ltd
4 Fitzhardinge Street
London W1H 0AH

Acknowledgements

I would like to thank the following for their help:
Angela ffrench for the line illustrations; Kathleen
Kinder and Mavis Walker for machine knitting sam-
ples 13, 17, 22, 28, 32 and 43; H.W. Peel and Co. Ltd
for producing special versions of their Chartwell True
Knit grids; and Alafoss, Avocet, Colinette, D.M.C.,
Jamieson & Smith, Rowan Yarns, Tiber, Lodge
Enterprises and 20th Century Yarns for providing
knitting and embroidery yarns.

Without the support of all those mentioned, it
would not have been such a pleasure to write this
book.

Abbreviations and Symbols

k	knit	I	knit
p	purl	−	purl
sl	slip		
st	stitch		
sts	stitches		

CONTENTS

PART ONE
HOW AND WHY
1 . . . AND WHAT

Embroidery on knitting. These three simple words conjure up a world of dazzling images. A plain piece of knitting is like a brand new canvas. On it, instead of paints and brushes, you can use colourful yarns and threads, cover it with cross stitch, duplicate the shape of the knitted stitches with Swiss darning, or work an abstract impression with free stitchery. Anything is possible on this soft, wonderful knitted canvas.

Embroidered knitting. A slight difference in words opens up a very different visual world. The canvas is no longer plain. The knitter's ability to create intriguing textures with little effort is revealed. Very simple embroidery then highlights, transforms or brings out the pattern in the knitting. It is a much more geometric world, just as dazzling as the other one, but totally different.

In the first instance, the knitting is just a perfectly ordinary piece of stocking stitch – knitted at home, or at a factory. It gives embroiderers a wonderful opportunity of displaying their skills, on a homemade or bought plain knitted garment. But knitters find the process far less appealing. Having had to keep their craft down to its most elementary level, they then have to struggle with the unfamiliar. An embroiderer might look forward to plotting a cross-stitch cockatoo right in the middle of a 150-stitch and 320-row back, or to bringing to life a garland of flowers with impromptu stitches. A knitter who is not an embroiderer too will tend to feel daunted by either prospect.

The knitter's difficulties can easily be solved. The knitting can be made more adventurous, even if it is only very slightly so. The embroidery can be made so simple that, although an experienced embroiderer might think that it lacks challenge, a knitter might get excited by the idea of trying it.

What follows is a voyage of discovery on the ways in which the two crafts can be made to blend. Although Italian and Spanish knitting, which occasionally use embroidery, formed the inspiration for some of the samples, most of the work in Part 2 is original and specially developed to show the tremendous possibilities of these techniques. This book is written by a knitter and for knitters – not necessarily experienced ones but, if nothing else, those familiar with the basics. Non-knitters, however, are welcome to join in. Although some technicalities might escape them, they can still enjoy applying the ideas to sweaters bought in a shop or made for them. If help is needed, a knitting friend can be called on to give a hand.

A big attraction of this kind of work is the way in which it uses colour. You can have any number of shades without constantly having to untangle the yarn spaghetti that you get in multi-coloured knitting. You knit with just one shade and add all the others later. This also allows you to introduce colour patterns that would otherwise be very awkward, and sometimes impossible, to knit successfully.

Adding embroidered colour to a knitted background has the further advantage that, if you have made a wrong choice, you can unpick just what you don't like, and quickly correct your error. When you are not very experienced, it is easy to use, say, pillar-box red instead of rose red. You may not realize your mistake until the work is finished, when you look at it objectively for the first time. In ordinary knitting, you would have to grit your teeth and unravel the whole thing, or go on pretending that it was not as bad as all that. In embroidered knitting, you simply unpick the offending red and replace it. Within a short time, your work looks perfect and you can feel proud of it. What more could you ask for?

From that great British institution, Marks and Spencer, comes this double-breasted, fitted cardigan in a fifty/fifty mohair and acrylic blend. The staggered columns of 'knit' stitches were crying out for a threaded running stitch, as used in Sample 11. However, mass-market production imposed some limitations. For example, the pattern was broken at the shoulders, and the seam lines were not as smooth as they might have been. Normally these things go unnoticed, but trying to decide which areas to embroider can make you rather pernickety.

Three yarns were chosen for the embroidery: thick chenille, glossy spun silk and a grainy wool and silk. Their forest colours and contrasting textures went particularly well with the rich, berry red of the sweater. They were used to produce two-colour triangles, juxtaposed so that the embroidery zigzags in panels down the fronts, the back and the sleeves. Finally, the seams around the neckband, the sleeve caps and the shoulders were emphasized with a stem stitch, worked quite straight so that all the small imperfections disappeared from view.

2 YARNS

If you are planning your own embroidered knitting, or any piece of knitting for which you don't want to follow a pattern published by a manufacturer or designer, start by choosing the yarns. Even if you have a rough idea of what you want to design – a wall hanging, a jacket to take the dog for a walk, a beach wrap or a dress for a special occasion – don't consider exact shapes or details until the chosen yarn is safely in the bag.

Buy a yarn only if you yearn to work with it. Judge its weight, its warmth, its softness, its colour. Consider how suitable it is for the purpose you have in mind, or imagine what it would be best used for. Look for other yarns that go well with it. They don't necessarily have to match it in fibre, thickness, texture or colour, so long as there is one common way of cleaning them safely.

Ideally, buy just one ball of the chosen yarn, or yarns, and return for the rest once you know exactly what you are going to do. Collect a few balls that look good together, including oddments – these can be very useful for the embroidery. Then start to play, combine and experiment. Hide the ball bands so that they don't distort the colours. Take one ball as the knitting colour and place strands of the other yarns on top of it. Add, remove and change the order of the strands.

As you play with the yarns, the colours will seem to change. Red, browns, blues, greens or yellows don't look the same in isolation as they do next to each other. This can be used to advantage. A vivid red, or a shocking pink, too bright to use on their own, can be toned down with cool pastels or soft neutrals. A muddy brown, or a dull beige, can be brought to life with vibrant jewel shades or primary colours.

Try many combinations, especially those that you would not normally use. You might have a notion that red doesn't go with green, or that blue doesn't go with brown. If you are only considering certain shades of these colours, you might well be right. But don't let your preconceived ideas stop you from trying to combine them, otherwise you will never see what a startling difference a slight variation in shade can make. Burnt orange might not go with pink until you find a certain pink and a certain burnt orange, or until you put a certain blue next to them.

YARN LIST

Many different kinds of yarn have been used to work the samples in Part Two. They have all been photographed full size, and can be seen on pages 11 and 13. Some of the yarns look very much alike, but have differences that, although small, alter their character and the way in which they should be used. Each yarn has been identified by a number, instead of a generic name, to avoid confusion with other yarns that might be given similar names by their manufacturers.

Plain wools

Wool makes warm and resilient yarns. If you stretch them, then release them, they regain their original state. For this reason, so long as the knitting tension is nicely firm, ribbings knitted in wool cause no problems, and garments keep their shape well.

1 A very fine tweed in pure new wool. The single thread is highly twisted. There is a variation in thickness and a certain crinkliness, both of which are reflected in the knitting. It has been used to knit sample 13.

2 This is the wool traditionally used in the Shetland Islands to knit their world-famous multicolour sweaters. Many yarns referred to as Shetland are not from the islands but this one is the real thing. It has a hint of roughness, its two threads are lightly spun and it is very warm. It should be knitted loosely because it plumps up when washed. It should then be dried stretched to shape, to avoid shrinkage. The soft colour is achieved by combining fibres treated with different dyes. Varying the proportion of the same dyes, or changing one of them, produces subtle differences that are easy to mix and match.

This yarn has been used to knit samples 28, 32, 35, and to embroider samples 8 and 42.

3 Like yarn 2, but self-coloured. In all, there are well over 100 shades of Shetland yarn, mostly very soft, but some unexpectedly bright. These are used in small amounts for accent, where a softer shade would simply sink into the background. They are very useful

This dark olive cardigan is a *Jeffrey Rogers* design, bought from a high street fashion shop. It is an attractive interpretation of a classic theme, knitted in fisherman's rib, a rather popular stitch among sweater manufacturers.

With its 100 per cent acrylic yarn and its amazingly low price, this was clearly not an 'heirloom'. There seemed little point in spending too many hours working on it. The embroidery, therefore, was limited to the lower front and the collar – which was just as well, since it soon became apparent why the price was so low. Two of the buttons were nowhere near to matching their buttonholes and, more seriously, one front was six ribs wider than the other.

To obtain a striking effect with little effort, the embroidery was executed in colourful, random-dyed chenille. The dash lines follow a technique not unlike the offset running stitch of Project 4. This time the needle is pushed horizontally through two consecutive ribs. The process is then repeated every third 'row'. In between groups of dash lines there is a line worked in four-sided stitch, also over two ribs and three 'rows'. To keep the top of the four-sided stitch lines on a level when the cardigan was worn, they had to be made increasingly longer towards the sides.

To plot the embroidery in cases such as this, where almost anything could be done, it is a good idea to outline the key areas with yarn or pins. Try the sweater on, have a critical look at it, and go on making adjustments until you are satisfied. Then start to embroider.

in certain kinds of embroidery, where the yarn is woven deep into the texture, or where only dots or thin lines of it are to be seen.

Self-coloured Shetland has been used to knit samples 17, 22, and to embroider samples 28, 32, 41 and 42.

4 This is probably the most popular of all knitting yarns, known in Britain as 'double knitting' – D.K. for short. It has four well-twisted threads, or plies, and is very smooth and even. Texture patterns knitted in D.K. show very clearly. Pure new wool has been used in this book, but many man-made wool imitations and blends are available. These are often cheaper and machine-washable (as is some wool), but in general don't breathe and are less warm. Ribbings may tend to lose their shape more easily when knitted in man-made fibres.

In embroidery, the yarn may become untwisted as you work. Turn the needle in your fingers to remedy this. D.K. has been used to knit samples 3, 24, 40, and to embroider sample 48.

Tapestry wool looks very similar to D.K. Although it is rarely used for knitting, it is well worth considering for the embroidery. It comes in literally hundreds of shades and very small skeins (some of the colours also come in large skeins), and is uniquely suited to two purposes. One is to find elusive shades not available in knitting yarns. The other is to grade your embroidery from light to dark in many smooth steps. Check whether it is washable or only dry cleanable when you buy it (see page 16).

Tapestry wool has been used to embroider samples 3, 17, 24, 40 and 48.

5 A pure D.K. wool with contrasting flecks. The flecks slightly blur the texture of the knitting, but add a certain playfulness. If you pick some of the fleck colours on the embroidery, you can't go wrong.

This yarn has been used to knit sample 7.

6 This is another well-known yarn: Aran wool. It is most commonly knitted in its natural off-white colour, but can be dyed in many shades, like the bright yellow shown here. It may look like a thicker D.K. but it only has three plies and is even more twisted and hard wearing. The cables and intricate patterns of the traditional Aran sweaters look as clear as they do because of the high twist of the wool. For the same reason, the knitting might be on the stiff and heavy side. In embroidery, the yarn might start to untwist.

Turn the needle in your fingers if that happens.

Aran wool has been used to knit sample 23.

7 A much thicker version of the single-ply wool tweed that heads this list. It is 'Aran weight', an expression often used to describe thickness. In fact, although the knitting tension might be similar to that given by an Aran yarn, this yarn is considerably lighter (there are 85m (93yd) in a 50g (2oz) ball, instead of only 75m (82yd) in Aran), and it doesn't give the same crispness of pattern. The uneven thickness, the crinkliness and the tweedy speckles combine to blur the stitch definition, giving a softer look.

This yarn has been used to embroider sample 37.

8 Like yarn 7, but chunkier. It has been used to knit sample 37.

9 Another chunky, single-ply wool, this time blended with 10 per cent mohair and given only a very slight twist. Thickness is also uneven but less so, and the yarn is much lighter (110m (120yd) in a 50g (2oz) ball in a yarn that, if anything, is thicker than Aran). The soft twist makes it very warm, because air is trapped. It also makes it fray and break easily when it is not knitted. If you are sewing or embroidering, keep moving the position of the needle and don't pull hard. For a more even thickness when embroidering, turn the needle in your fingers when reaching a thick area.

This yarn has been used to knit samples 9, 30, and to embroider samples 11, 15, 25 and 35.

There is another yarn that looks very much like this one in short lengths. It is a softer yarn, being a blend of 55 per cent wool and 45 per cent alpaca, and it gradually changes colour over a matter of rows. It has been used to knit sample 18.

10 This is lopi, the traditional pure wool from Iceland. It is spun like yarn 9, but is considerably thicker. It has been used to knit samples 12, 21, and to embroider samples 21, 35 and 47.

11 Like yarn 10, but speckled. It has been used to knit sample 47 and to embroider samples 21 and 35.

12 Not really a yarn, but a wool roving from which a yarn would normally be spun. It is hand dyed in gentle colour variations. Rovings are rarely used to knit with, but don't dismiss them. Powerful embroidery effects can be obtained with little effort, as can be seen in sample 12.

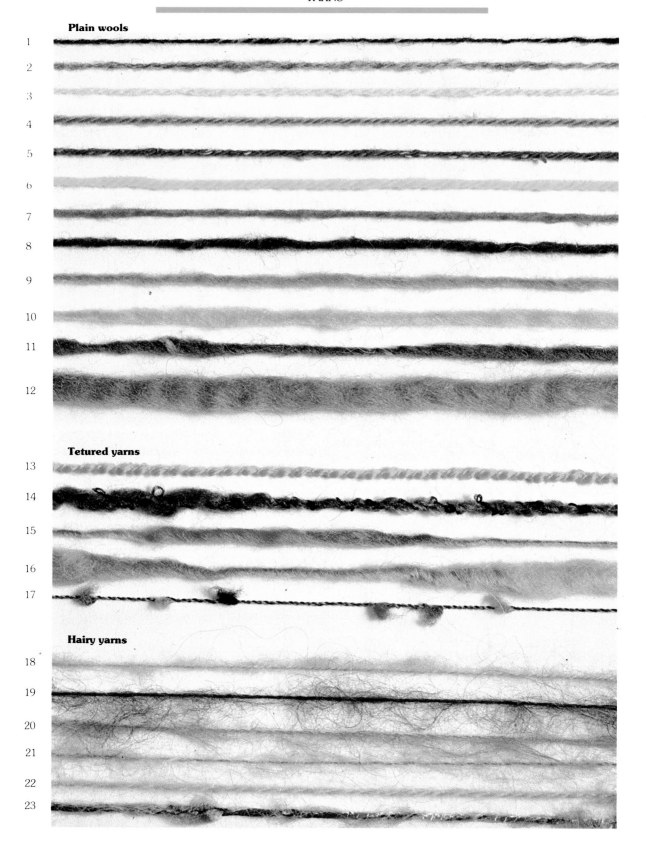

Plain wools

1
2
3
4
5
6
7
8
9
10
11
12

Tetured yarns

13
14
15
16
17

Hairy yarns

18
19
20
21
22
23

Textured yarns

If a yarn is given some sort of texture, the knitting is bound to reflect it. The stitches will be less clear and may become distorted. In the case of slub yarns with thin, well-twisted areas and thick, untwisted areas, some stitches turn out to be much larger and tighter than others. In embroidery, make sure that anything a slub yarn has to go through is large enough for the thickest areas, and keep the needle where the yarn is thinnest.

Any lumps in a texture yarn will tend to stay on the purl side, where the yarn travels from stitch to stitch but doesn't actually go into any stitches.

13 In this case, a very fine and firmly spun thread has been wound around a thick and softly spun thread, producing a spiral yarn in pure new wool with a crinkly texture. It has been used to knit sample 25.

14 This is an interesting wool and acrylic blend. There is so much going on in it, in terms of colour, texture and thickness, that the knitted pattern has little chance of showing – as can be seen in the illustration on page 19. It has been used to knit sample 15 and to embroider sample 22.

15 A straightforward slub yarn in pure new wool. Its main attraction is the way in which it has been hand dyed in a multitude of bold shades. It has been used to knit samples 8, 27, and to embroider sample 23.

16 Similar to yarn 15, but much thicker and slubbier. It has been used to knit sample 38.

17 A very fine and highly twisted polyamide yarn with confetti-like blobs of fibres. This is one of those novelty yarns that come and go in fashion, but seems an excellent example for demonstrating how to handle the unexpected. It has been used to knit sample 41.

Hairy yarns

These can often be knitted much more loosely than is generally accepted for plain yarns. The hairs fill the gaps between the stitches and prevent them from losing their shape. They also, however, prevent the knitted texture from showing very clearly.

Brushed mohair is the most popular of hairy yarns. It is often thought of as being a standard type of yarn, with each brand having similar qualities. This is not the case. Some yarns are so much thinner than others that interchanging them would be very unwise. Fibre composition also varies, affecting both the yarn character and its weight.

The pile of all hairy yarns can be raised with a stiff brush or teasel after work is completed. A sumptuous fuzzy cloud will result. The pattern will show even less than usual through the cloud, so keep it very simple if you want the delicate furry effect.

18 This particular mohair yarn is very fine and one of the softest available, although is not as warm as others. Kid mohair accounts for 80 per cent of it, and the remaining 20 per cent is chlorofibre. It has been used to knit samples 4 and 39.

19 A much thicker and warmer mohair, not as soft as yarn 18 but with masses of very long hairs. It is a blend of 78 per cent mohair, 13 per cent wool and 9 per cent nylon. It has been used to knit sample 44.

20 Pure brushed mohair is not widely manufactured, but this is an example of it. In thickness and warmth it falls between yarns 18 and 19, but closer to 19. The hairs are very lustrous and, although it looks so delicate, it is extremely tough and doesn't need washing too often because it repels dirt. It has been used to embroider sample 18.

21 It is not mohair this time, but brushed lustre wool, hand dyed in gently varying shades. It is very thick and warm, and has been used to embroider samples 9 and 27.

22 Angora is one of the softest fibres used in knitting, but it is not very popular as it keeps shedding its hairs, both during knitting and afterwards. It is very difficult to spin by itself. This particular example has 50 per cent angora, 25 per cent wool and 25 per cent acrylic. It has been used to embroider samples 26 and 45.

23 There is some mohair in this yarn, but only 15 per cent. The rest is divided between viscose (the space-dyed ribbon) and acrylic fibres. The yarn has such a rich texture, that it blurs much of the detail in the knitting, so choose a simple stitch. Embroidery effects, on the other hand, can be very effective and quick to achieve. The yarn has been used to knit and embroider sample 16 and to knit sample 45.

Silks

Silk is certainly the most luxurious of all fibres used in knitting or embroidery. Although silk yarns are warm, they can also be heavy and not very resilient. Ribbings go on spreading, so you might as well avoid them.

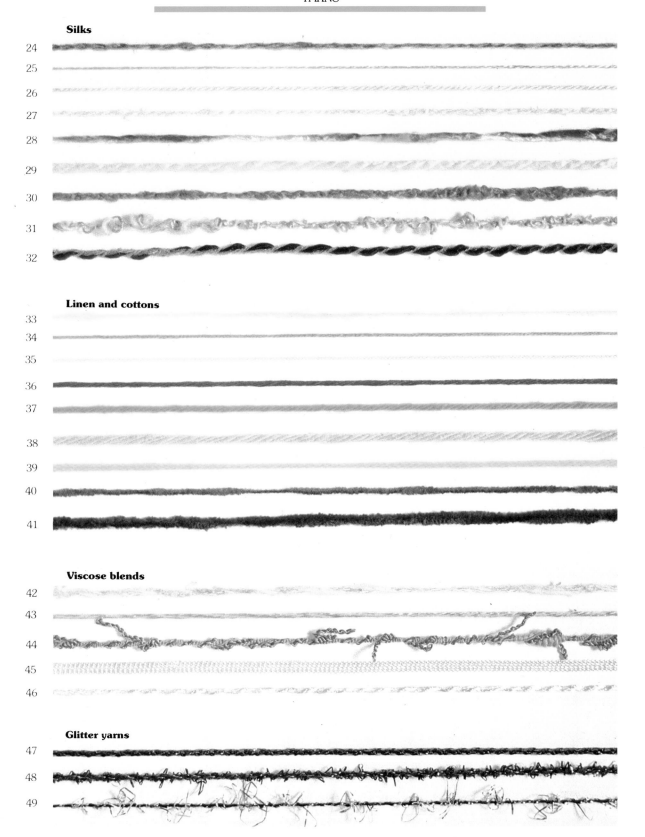

Silks

24

25

26

27

28

29

30

31

32

Linen and cottons

33

34

35

36

37

38

39

40

41

Viscose blends

42

43

44

45

46

Glitter yarns

47

48

49

Garments tend to droop and lose their shape unless firmly knitted – watch your tension.

The glossier silks are very slippery. Dropped stitches tend to unravel very quickly. If you do drop one, don't stretch the knitting sideways, or it will unravel even faster.

24 This silk yarn has been blended with 48 per cent wool, which makes it warmer and also more resilient; ribbings in this yarn are more inclined to recover their original shape. The tweedy speckles also make it less formal than a glossy spun silk. The colours can be picked up in the embroidery very successfully. It has been used to knit samples 14, 31 and 43.

25 A very fine, well-twisted, pure, spun silk, hand dyed in delicate shade variations. It has been used to knit sample 33.

26 Silk and wool again, as in yarn 24, but this time more tightly twisted, with no flecks, and hand dyed by the same method as yarn 25. It has been used to embroider sample 6.

27 The coarser silk fibres are also used in yarn spinning. They are less lustrous, less slippery, lighter, more affordable and also very attractive. This example has been used to knit and embroider sample 10.

28 A single, barely twisted pure silk thread, hand dyed in contrasting shades. It is a knitting yarn very well suited to embroidery, as can be seen in samples 13 and 31.

29 Pure silk at its most luxurious. This thick yarn and the three that follow have been produced on a small-scale twisting machine, under the vigilant eye of a craftsman/designer. It is also hand dyed, and has been used to embroider samples 19 and 29.

30 This intriguing blend of spun silk and Tussah silk, with its crunchy texture, comes from the same source as yarn 29. Like most silks it is heavy, but the rough surface makes it more manageable than usual. It has been used to knit sample 6 and to embroider sample 38.

31 A loop yarn blending wool with 45 per cent silk, made as explained for yarn 29. The knitted texture will be hardly visible because the yarn itself has such a rich texture, so keep it simple. It has been used to knit sample 26.

32 This is the last one of four yarns produced in the same way as yarn 29. A soft core of spun silk has been wrapped with fine worsted-wool threads. It has been used to embroider samples 36 and 44.

Linen and cottons

These are much cooler yarns than wool. They are similarly comfortable but much heavier and less resilient. Ribbings wear well in cuffs, necklines and jacket waistbands if they are firmly knitted, but lose their shape very quickly if the tension is on the slack side. Waistband ribbings in jumpers might work well if they are intended to be loose fitting. A waistband meant to gather the jumper at the waist will either be too narrow to get the jumper over the head and shoulders, or be stretched with the effort.

Because these fibres become very heavy when washed, and then take a long time to dry, they are often mixed with acrylics. The resulting blend is lighter and much easier to look after, but is not as cool.

Mercerized cotton, because of its high gloss, can be rather slippery.

33 This is a single-ply, slightly rough, linen yarn. It is somewhat uneven in thickness, with occasional hairs sticking out. It has been used to embroider samples 39 and 46.

34 Stranded, mercerized embroidery cotton, like tapestry wool, comes in small skeins and hundreds of shades. Similarly, it is excellent for working dark-to-light effects, and for toning in to perfection with the knitting yarn. Take care to keep an even twist by turning the needle with your fingers every now and then. Don't dry clean (see page 16).

Stranded cotton has been used to embroider samples 14 and 30.

35 This cabled yarn is another example of mercerized cotton. Eight very fine threads are plied, first in pairs and then together, to give a very even and smooth yarn. The knitted texture shows in great detail, because of both yarn construction and the way the surface reflects light. It has been used to embroider samples 7 and 43.

36 Six single threads have been loosely spun together to produce a soft all-cotton yarn. The knitted pattern shows well but lacks the crispness given by yarn 35. It has been used to knit sample 46.

37 This sample shows a traditional double-knitting yarn, which has been spun in cotton instead of wool, as yarn 4 was. It gives the clear texture expected of D.K. yarns. It has been used to knit and embroider sample 20 and to knit sample 34.

38 This very chunky, soft cotton has five plies. It gives good, clear stitches, and has been used to knit sample 11.

39 Most knitting yarns are spun, but this one has actually been knitted. If you find the fine cotton thread and pull it, the yarn unravels. You can then see that the yarn is really a stocking-stitch tube, flattened during packaging, so that it looks like a somewhat uneven and narrow ribbon. It has been used to embroider sample 46.

40 Chenille is like a knittable velvet. It is sometimes produced as an acrylic blend, but this example is all cotton. The pile of the yarn blurs the outline of the knitted stitches but, on the other hand, makes purl stitches or slip stitches stand out boldly on a background of knit stitches. In embroidery, long strands should be kept untwisted, unless an even, high-twist effect is sought. It has been used to knit sample 5.

41 This is a thicker version of yarn 40. It has been used to knit samples 36 and 42, and to embroider samples 9, 18 and 26.

Viscose blends

Viscose rayon is used for its shiny look, rather like silk but at a fraction of the price. It is quite heavy too but, unlike silk, it is cold to the touch.

Yarns 23, 47 and 46 are also viscose blends.

42 This is a very loosely spun blend of 56 per cent cotton, 36 per cent viscose and 8 per cent silk. It has an interesting, somewhat slubby texture which shows in the knitting. It has been used to embroider sample 5.

43 For this yarn, 60 per cent viscose and 40 per cent cotton have been loosely twisted together into four fine threads, later plied. The two-stage process results in a mottled matt-and-shiny appearance, and a quite clear knitted texture. It has been used to knit and embroider sample 1, and to embroider samples 26 and 34.

44 This is a yarn with a fascinating texture. It is a blend of 54 per cent viscose, 28 per cent cotton, 15 per cent acrylic and 3 per cent polyamide. When knitted, the little tails tend to stay on the purl side. When embroidering, you might have some difficulty making the yarn go through tight spots. It has been used to embroider sample 20.

45 Like yarn 39, this is a knitted yarn. Unlike it, it is quite wide, very heavy and slippery and more clearly like a ribbon. It is made up of 88 per cent viscose and 12 per cent nylon. When knitting a ribbon yarn you have to decide whether to take it as it comes, or emphasize its structure. The second choice means that you have to keep untwisting it as you knit. This is rather tedious and hardly worth the effort if you want plain stocking stitch. However, keeping the ribbon untwisted can make textured patterns look much more three-dimensional than they would normally do. Even garter stitch and the purl side of stocking stitch acquire an unexpected sculptured quality. In embroidery, long strands are best kept untwisted, or given a uniform twist.

Knitted ribbon has been used to knit sample 2 and to embroider samples 4 and 18.

46 To make this yarn two viscose, knitted ribbons, not unlike yarn 45 but much narrower, have been wrapped together with a very fine mother-of-pearl thread. Because one of the ribbons is darker than the other, the glossy yarn seems to be changing colour. It has been used to embroider sample 4.

Glitter yarns

These festive, playful yarns are not always the easiest to work with, but they are too wonderful to be excluded from a journey into pattern and texture. Don't expect the knitted stitches to show much, if at all, and remember that the yarn texture will show better on the purl side.

47 This yarn looks rather like a chain and has a nice, smooth surface. A thin, glossy thread makes it sparkle. The blend contains 75 per cent viscose and 25 per cent polyamide. It has been used to knit sample 29.

48 There are three plies in this yarn, each one of which has a thin polyamide thread wrapped over a wool (75 per cent) and metallic polyester (22 per cent) core. The wool has been kept smooth while the polyester crinkles in and out of the core, making the yarn look spiky. The high wool content makes it much lighter and warmer than most glitter yarns. It has been used to embroider sample 33.

49 Wearing something made in this witty tinsel could

easily bring you into competition with the Christmas tree. It is not unlike a single-ply version of yarn 49, but the metallic polyester threads are in two colours and much wilder. There is less wool (51 per cent) and more metallic polyester and polyamide (38 and 11 per cent), but the yarn remains light and warm. It has been used to knit sample 19, and to embroider sample 2.

CLEANING YARNS

All branded knitting yarns come with cleaning or washing instructions. Unbranded yarns can often be hand washed, but knit and wash a sample before starting to work with them. Embroidery cottons and tapestry wools carry no information on the little skeins. Recommendations from a leading manufacturer have been included in the yarn list, but check with your supplier to make sure.

As a general rule, it is a good idea to wash or dry clean a fully-embroidered sample before finally deciding on yarns and stitches, even if the embroidery yarn matches the knitting yarn. If it doesn't, compare the different cleaning recommendations, and follow the procedure which is gentlest.

3 YARNS AND STITCHES

Having gathered a selection of yarns that go well together, you have to select knitting and embroidery stitches, and make a final choice of yarns. The aim must be to find the knitting stitch that will show the knitting yarn at its best while allowing for the kind of embroidery that will display the embroidery yarn effectively. The idea is to make the most of the qualities of the yarn and compensate for its drawbacks. If a yarn has an interesting structure (probably what attracted you to it in the first place) the stitches chosen should emphasize the structure, rather than conceal it.

At the end of the book there are 48 samples of embroidered knitting. Take them as examples or starting points. Don't be tempted to begin by looking at them with the idea of finding yarns to match them later. Either the yarns or the shades used could be out of production and, in desperation, you might buy yarns only half-matching the original – which might be unsuitable for the knitting or embroidery stitches involved. The resulting flop would not be much of an incentive to try again.

The notes on knitting and embroidery yarns in this section give some idea of what to expect from different yarn types. They might help you select two or three samples, out of the 48, to try with your own yarns. Or, perhaps, you could test the same sample in two or three yarn combinations, until you find the one that looks just right.

If you prefer to do things your own way, select the yarns first, and then choose a knitting stitch and see how it could be enhanced with embroidery. Alternatively, pick first an embroidery stitch and work out what kind of knitting pattern it requires.

If you have never experimented before, don't be afraid to take the plunge. It is far easier, far more enjoyable and far more satisfying than trying to match or adapt someone else's ideas. Get yourself one of those books brimming with illustrations of knitting stitches. The first time you look at one of them, the idea of selecting two or three stitches out of the hundreds they contain sounds like looking for the needle in the proverbial haystack. Fortunately, the pictures can be scanned very quickly by simply applying a little common sense.

If, for instance, you know that the texture of the fabric is not going to show very distinctly because the knitting yarn is hairy or textured, dismiss all the stitches with long or awkward instructions. If the yarn is spaced dyed, search for stitches in which the rows encroach on each other. If the embroidery yarn is very knobbly and would be difficult to pull through ordinary knitting stitches, look only for patterns with eyelets, long loops or strands across the fabric, or anything else the yarn can easily be taken through. If you want a fabric that is not going to curl, try to find a balanced combination of knit and purl stitches.

YARNS FOR KNITTING

Have a good look at the knitting yarn first and see what can be expected from it.

With a **heavy yarn** you must avoid patterns that make very thick fabrics, unless you are planning something horizontal. The weight will make any vertical project sag, especially if the yarn is also slippery, like silk or viscose. Heavy yarns need stitches with smooth surfaces and/or holes, elongated loops made by wrapping the yarn two or three times around the needle, or loose areas kept under control by firm areas.

If you use a **hairy yarn** the pattern will show more or less clearly, depending on the amount and type of fuzzy fibres there are. With a very hairy yarn, if you brush the knitting afterwards the pattern may practically disappear. Some instructions, like 'pass slip-stitch over', will be difficult to work because the hairs will get caught. Avoid instructions such as these.

If you have a **smooth yarn** with a strong twist, you can be sure that the knitted stitches will show clearly, especially if the yarn is pale and glossy. Therefore, if you feel like working a complex pattern, your efforts will be rewarded.

Green, wool-blend jumper from a fashion chain-store, embroidered with crinkly cotton yarn (full details page 41)

Peach-coloured wool-blend sweater from an Italian chain-store, embroidered in three shades of Shetland wool (full details see page 37)

If, on the other hand, you have a **textured yarn**, to work a complex pattern would be a waste of time. If the yarn was knobbly, it could also be pretty awkward. Textured yarns require simple patterns, but don't turn automatically to stocking stitch. This may be a simple pattern, but it usually flattens the texture of the yarn, which is precisely what needs to be emphasized. Look instead for patterns with very short instructions, patterns that you can knit automatically, but which have some texture. This can be purl stitches on a knit background (very easy examples of this being moss stitch or occasional purl rows), patterns with horizontal bars across slipped stitches, brioche patterns that work some stitches into the row below, or even garter stitch or stocking stitch used on the purl side.

The way in which the yarn has been dyed should have a very similar bearing on your choice. **Self-coloured yarns** show the knitting clearly. **Spaced-dyed yarns** don't, because the pattern made by the colours conflicts with the pattern made by the stitches. Very often, if you work in stocking stitch, these yarns settle to a zebra kind of arrangement, or to zigzagging vertical stripes. The free blending of the colours, so appealing before you start to knit, is lost. By comparison, the yarn now looks crude and unattractive. The reverse side of stocking stitch tends to give a better picture, because all the rows overlap, and the stretches of colour intermingle – especially if you use it sideways. But there are other tricks at hand to liven things up, like slipping some stitches for one or more rows (either leaving the bars at front or at back of work), or using patterns with constant decreases and increases along the rows. Either of these techniques could be on a mainly purl background, for extra colour blending. With a fine yarn, you could also blend the colours by working two or more strands together.

Different effects obtained with yarn 14 (pages 11 and 12). From top to bottom: knit side of stocking stitch; moss stitch; wasp's nest stitch; fisherman's rib (on an odd number of stitches, right-side rows: knit; wrong-side rows: *p1, k the st below next st, then drop the next st from left needle, repeat from *, p1); garter stitch; purl side of stocking stitch.

KNITTED FABRICS

After considering the knitting yarn, and cutting down the number of possible stitches accordingly, start thinking about what you want to knit. Some knitted fabrics are very flat, most have a clear curl even after careful blocking, and a few curl so much that they can be put successfully to only a limited number of uses. Depending on what you want to do, some patterns will be best avoided.

Fabrics with a **knit background**, and especially stocking stitch, curl out at top and bottom and in at the sides. Fabrics with a **purl background** curl in the opposite way: in at top and bottom, and out at the sides. You can use the curling tendency to advantage, by leaving some of the edges to turn into a roll. Alternatively, you can correct it by adding a band in a flat stitch. Hems are another possibility, but these require all sorts of devices to make them look neat.

If you opt for adding flat bands to the two fronts of a coat or jacket with a knit background, your body will keep the bands in position. The simple fact of being worn prevents a fabric with a knit base from curling in. If the fabric has a purl base, unless you keep the jacket buttoned up at all times, the two fronts will fold back on themselves – taking with them the flat band, however wide this is. An easy solution to this problem is to knit the jacket from side to side. The front edges will then curl in, and the problem will be there no more. To correct an already finished jacket, try the blocking technique on page 73.

A **flat fabric** has an even mixture of knit and purl stitches – the pull of the knits is balanced by the pull of the purls. Common flat fabrics are moss stitch; k1, p1 or k2, p2 ribbings; and garter stitch. Note that what matters is, not so much what you knit, as what you see from the right side. If you work back and forth in rows, garter stitch is 'knit all stitches of all rows'. What you knit from the wrong side, on the return rows, however, shows like purl on the right side. This makes garter stitch really 'knit one row, purl one row' – exactly what needs to be done in circular knitting. An all-over flat fabric is required for projects that need to hang straight.

YARNS FOR EMBROIDERY

Yarns that are easy to work with in knitting are often troublesome in embroidery, and vice versa. Some

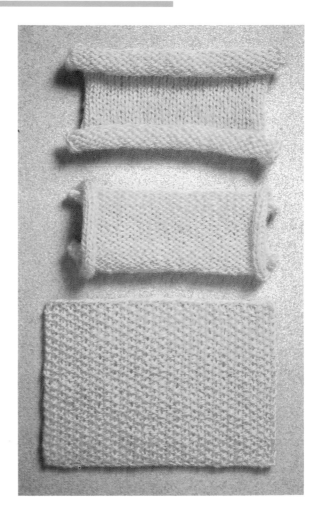

Knit fabrics curl out at top and bottom and in at the sides. Purl fabrics curl in the opposite way. Fabrics with an even mixture of knit and purl, such as moss stitch, remain flat.

yarns, however, cause problems only with some stitches, not with others.

Look at any embroidery stitches in the light of whichever yarns you would like to use. Shortlist a few that look appealing and unlikely to cause unnecessary problems. If you started with several possible embroidery yarns, now is the time to start weeding them out.

Take a strand of yarn in your hands and see what happens when you give it a couple of turns, one way or the other. This will give you an idea of how embroidering will affect yarn twist.

Plied smooth yarns often untwist or become more twisted as you embroider. You should not dismiss them because of this, but be aware that a little more effort will be necessary. Stitches that show long stretches of yarn are worst affected. Perfection might be unattainable because many yarns have little flaws of their own, but a beady eye should be kept on the twist as work progresses. Turning the needle with the fingers is enough to restore the original twist. Often a pattern can be established, such as giving the needle 'half a clockwise turn after every stitch'.

Textured yarns present fewer problems. Because of their more complex nature, twist changes caused by the embroidery could well go unnoticed.

Ribbon tends to look best when kept flat. An even, high twist might be worth considering on occasions. Either effect means taking some trouble while working, turning the needle as required.

Chenille also looks best either untwisted or highly twisted, if the stitches are long. If they are short there is far less need to fuss over the twist, especially if two or more of them cross, or are laid very close to each other.

Slub yarns tend to produce interesting thick and thin effects. These sometimes settle into a rhythm matching the pattern made by the knitting. The only thing to make sure of is that the knitting has holes, or strands across the surface, for the thick, slubby areas to go through.

Bold lines of embroidery can be obtained with **thin yarns** in several ways. One way is to do several rows of embroidery close together, perhaps mirroring the slant of the stitches if they have one, and perhaps changing the shade of the yarn. Another way is to work one stitch on top of another – some stitches go very well together, either in the same or contrasting shades. A third way is to choose stitches that give double or multiple lines in preference to those that give a single line. For example, chain stitch makes two lines, backstitch only one. Another way of emboldening a thin yarn is to use two or more strands together. With certain stitches, working with a double strand is rather like working with ribbon – the two strands need to be kept untwisted if the effect is to be consistent. Running stitch is a very good example of this. However, it is often possible to work with six or eight strands without too much worry.

Spaced-dyed yarns can produce startling effects with little effort. It is well worth giving them a try.

4 EMBROIDERY

When trying to think of a way to embroider a knitted fabric, look at its structure. Changes of pattern, holes, purl stitches, loops, grooves etc, can all be put to good use. The samples at the end of the book make clear how this can be done.

When it comes to embroidering, there are four main types of knitting stitches:
- those with a very definite structure;
- those giving an all-over pattern that, although clear, can be picked up in diverse ways;
- those that simply provide a useful grid;
- and those which are best left alone, because they are either nondescript or sufficiently decorative.

The **first group** includes texture stripes, cables, insertions, seams worked with embroidery in mind, and any other pattern that makes a definite statement. The structure of this kind of stitch is so clear that the best thing to do is go along with it and emphasize it. Working against the structure reduces the effect and lessens the impact. However, there might be different ways of interpreting the stitch. In dealing with cables, for example, the way in which they travel should be highlighted, but this can be achieved by emphasizing either the 'ropes' (as in samples 32 and 34), or the background (as in samples 36 and 35).

The **second group** includes knit-and-purl patterns (especially brocades, with their geometric or figurative themes), and stitches with repeating units that neither make a grid nor have enough character to belong to the first group. Sometimes, patterns become part of this group merely because of their size when knitted. If they are worked with fine yarn and needles they belong to the second group – the repeats are too small and numerous to make an individual impact. If they are worked with thick yarn and needles, however, or if the pattern is somehow enlarged to accommodate the original number of stitches and rows several times over, they become part of the first group; increasing their size makes the repeats much bolder.

Stitches belonging to the second group offer a number of options. Highlight each repeat (as in samples 11 and 33). Highlight certain lines only (as in sample 14). Establish a regular sequence of highlighting (as in sample 22). Outline occasional repeats to reveal an unsuspected pattern (as in samples 13 and 15). Change the overall impression (as in samples 23 and 24 – started with distinctive vertical zigzags).

The **third group** includes stitches with a regular texture that can be used as a grid. Garter stitch (samples 10 and 42), moss stitch (samples 1 to 4) and wasp's nest stitch (samples 21 and 25) are good examples of small grids. Although they may not look like much, grids are very directional. Geometric patterns can be built up quickly and easily. Even inexperienced knitters and embroiderers can achieve wonderful woven effects.

A larger kind of grid is provided by regularly distributing single eyelets on a stocking stitch fabric (as in samples 16 to 20).

The **fourth group** gathers all the stitches that don't fit in any of the others. Some knitted fabrics just don't lend themselves easily to embroidery and are best left alone. Some are so intricate that there is no room for successful addition. Others are so plain that they give no pointers as to how to build a pattern over them.

Stocking stitch exemplifies the last kind of fabric. The individual stitches are so much of a muchness that they can't be said to make a grid. Stocking stitch is more like the woven fabrics used for counted-thread embroidery. It is perfect for 'embroidery on knitting', but no good for 'embroidered knitting'. However, when spiced up with other stitches, it can be put to certain uses. Rows with regularly spaced purl stitches can outline a stripe (as in sample 7). A ribbed border can provide a good starting point for vertical lines (as in samples 37 and 39).

Once the lines have been spaced with the help of a border, as in the example mentioned above, to follow a stitch path *across* rows of stocking stitch presents little difficulty. To follow a stitch path *along* a row is more of a challenge. It is easy to lose track of the row you want and move to the one above or below. A little trick overcomes this problem, and then the embroidery can be made to reflect textured stripes introduced at the knitting stage (as in sample 5). The trick is worked while knitting: having just completed the row to be embroidered, and with this row still on the needle, work a running stitch on the row below; go into one stitch and come up on the next one, using a fine and contrasting yarn or thread. This gives the

Blue jumper – hand knitted and embroidered in cotton (full details page 35)

Orange jumper – hand-knitted in mohair and embroidered in chenille (full details page 39)

clearest possible guide for embroidering. It is done one row down to prevent the running stitch interfering with the embroidery.

TECHNICALITIES

Needles

Use only tapestry needles, or sewing needles especially designed for knitting, with really blunt points. These can be bought in several sizes. Try to build up a good selection, and choose whichever is most appropriate for the job in hand. To thread the yarn, bend it into a 'U'. If you can't get the 'U' through the eye without wetting it, the needle is too thin. Thin needles are difficult to work with; they also fray the yarn, spoiling the work.

Pinning down

To keep the embroidery at exactly the right tension, and to avoid crumpling the knitting, try securing the work to a large, flat surface. This could be a board, a firm cushion or a mattress. The knitting can be kept in place with a few large pins. Because your needle will have a blunt point, it is unlikely to catch threads from the board or cushion covering. If, however, this has a very loose weave, put a smooth cloth between the covering and the knitting.

Blocking

Always block the knitting before starting to embroider to give it its true size. Pin your unsewn knitted pieces right side up, and then spray them with cold water. In this way there is no risk of crushing the texture or scorching the fibres. Use the longest glass-headed pins you can find, and as many of them as necessary to stop the edges from peaking. Stretch the knitting just very slightly, until the smallest crease has disappeared. Raise the texture, if any, with your fingers or with the end of a cable or knitting needle. Dampen it quite well with a plant sprayer and keep it flat until it dries. If necessary, block again after embroidering.

Tension

Always make a tension square before you start to knit. Block it, embroider it, and then count the stitches and rows in 10cm (4in.). This can only be done accurately if the square is fractionally larger, because the edges must be kept out of the count. The tension can

change dramatically once the embroidery has been added. If the embroidery is such that it will add stability, or fill many of the knitted stitches, you might need to knit at a looser tension than you would under ordinary circumstances.

Don't ignore warnings on tension and blocking just because you have read them many times. Not to make a tension square is daft, because it is the only means of knowing that the size you are knitting is the size you want. Blocking is equally essential, and the method recommended gives excellent results. When properly done, it can be difficult to believe that the piece of knitting unpinned at the end, is the same one that was originally pinned.

Seams

Seams are mostly sewn after embroidering. Using a ladder stitch is the neatest way of sewing an ordinary

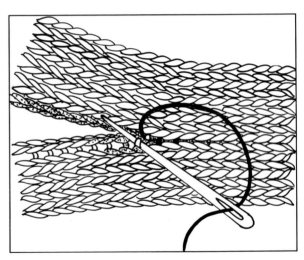

Ladder-stitch seam

seam. Work with right side facing, and without tacking, but do make sure that you have the same number of rows on both sides. Catch the horizontal bar between the two edge stitches with the needle. Repeat it on the other side. Keep alternating the sides. That is all. If you have two cast-off ends, catch either a half or a whole stitch each time, just below the chain line. If you have a side edge and a cast-off edge, attach one to the other with safety pins without overlapping, to make sure that one of them doesn't pucker. Catch the horizontal bar from the side edge in the usual way, then catch only as much as you need from the cast-off edge to keep the two sides even.

If a seam is too bulky, pin it well all along its length. Spray it until it is quite damp and then let it dry.

Starting to work

Anchor the embroidery yarns securely, by weaving them to-and-fro along the edge, or on the wrong side. Don't use knots. These would go through the fabric and appear on the right side.

Hiding yarn tails into seams

When running many lines of stitches close together, it might be an idea to cut the yarn long enough to go from one end to the other. When planning a design, consider working from end to end with manageable lengths of yarn. If the idea proves feasible, the yarns need be anchored by only one or two backstitches at either end. The yarn tails will form an untidy fringe, to be secured and enclosed within a special seam or edge trimming. A stocking-stitch edge left to roll of its own accord, then lightly stitched, is ideal for the purpose. So is a flat-felled seam, with its two overlapping layers. Blocking corrects much of the resulting stiffness. The seam will be bulkier than usual but, so long as it has been correctly integrated within the design, this should not be a deterrent.

Keeping all the yarn tails at the ends and then hiding them is especially appropriate when the embroidery shows only on the right side of work. There are quite a number of situations when all that can be seen on the wrong side are yarn joins. By restricting these to the ends, the wrong side looks immaculate.

Time factors

Although embroideries covering most of the knitted surface always look very time consuming, some of them can be done quite quickly. How long something takes depends on how easy it is to work, as well as on how much of it there is. Embroidering the tension square gives a very good idea of what to expect.

Time is sometimes saved by not trying to save it. There are cases (running stitch is the clearest of them), in which pulling the yarn after every stitch may seem a waste of time. Pulling it only at the end of the line, or after every three or four needle movements, looks like a good time saver. What that does, in fact, is to increase the tension of most of the stitches to an unacceptable level. It then takes ages to loosen them all evenly.

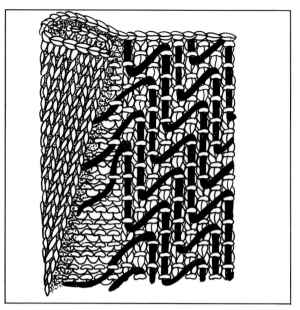

Stocking-stitch edge roll

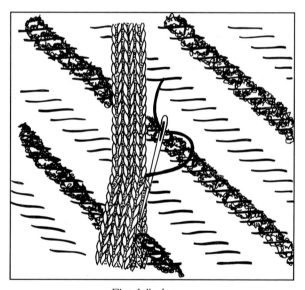

Flat-felled seam

Correcting yarn twist

If at any time the embroidery yarn becomes too twisted, or starts to untwist, turn the needle with your fingers. This will restore the yarn to its original state.

If you are working with ribbon or chenille, either keep it untwisted or give it a strong, even twist. If you are working with two strands of yarn, keep them untwisted so that they stay parallel – at least on the visible areas. Make sure that one doesn't pull more than the other.

Adding emphasis

If you want to add to the impact made by a certain stitch, you have a few choices. Work several lines of embroidery close together, perhaps changing shade and/or mirroring the stitch if this has a slant (as in sample 43). Overlap two lines (as in sample 46). Work a different stitch on top of the first one (as in samples 38 and 45). Work many lines of the same stitch, perhaps in different shades, to build up an intricate pattern (as in sample 47).

Colour

To emphasize depth, use dark shades (as in samples 11, 33 and 41). To emphasize height, use pale shades (as in sample 34). To change the character of the knitted texture, use pale or bright shades in low areas (as in sample 9 and 14), dark shades on high areas. To make a deeply woven pattern show, use high contrasts (as in samples 25 and 42).

STITCHES

The embroidery stitches used in Part Two are mainly very easy. In fact, the one most often used is the simplest of all – running stitch. In general, it is best to insert the needle into the centre of a knitted stitch, or in between stitches. These are usually quite easy to see, which is a great advantage when it comes to ensuring that all the embroidery stitches are of the same size. All you have to do is decide whether the embroidery stitches should be one, two, three, etc. knitted-stitches long, and then bring the needle up or down accordingly. Pull the yarn until it lays flat and straight, but not tight.

Running stitch

This is the easiest stitch. In essence, it is like a tacking or darning stitch. Bring needle down at 1 and up at 2, going through the fabric as in the illustration, or simply burrowing under any bumps you see

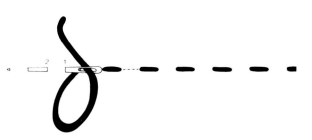

on the surface – purl stitches, for example. Normally, the stitch travels from right to left, but a knitted fabric makes work so much easier than a woven one, that you can perfectly well work it from top to bottom, or from bottom to top, if you prefer. Use it for horizontal, vertical or diagonal lines. These, by the way, can be combined or offset to create stepped effects. Patterns based on pattern-darning embroidery, or the old huckaback embroidery, can often be adapted.

Running stitch has been used in samples 1, 9, 10, 12, 18, 19, 25, 31, 34, 35, 36 and 42. The stepped version has been used in samples 3 and 4.

Threaded running stitch

The original version of this requires a foundation running stitch. This is threaded up and down with the same yarn, or with a different one. A second threading, covering the gaps left by the first, can be added. In embroidered knitting, as well as a running stitch, anything that makes a raised line (or a line of spaced, raised stitches) can be used as a foundation. A grid such as moss stitch, also makes a good foundation – horizontal or diagonal lines can be followed. Embroidery stitches other than running stitch (chain stitch, backstitch or cross stitch, for example), can also be considered, as can double, rather than single lines.

Threaded running stitch has been used in samples 2, 11, 26 and 38.

Whipped running stitch

This is another way of threading a foundation of running stitches in embroidery – or, in embroidered knitting, any foundation that lends itself to being threaded in this way. A whipping stitch can also be used in other situations. For example, it can move in and out of the holes of an eyelet grid.

Whipped running stitch has been used in samples 21 and 34. Whipping has been used in samples 17 and 40. Notice that this stitch can be mirrored, and that when two mirrored lines are placed against each other, the result looks rather like zigzag backstitch.

Satin stitch

In embroidery, this stitch is used for filling. The stitches are vertical in the illustration, but they could be slanted. Work from right to left, or from left to right. Bring the needle down at 1, up at 2, very close to the last stitch made – the background should be well covered. Satin stitch is easiest to work if you follow a change-in-pattern line, and if you space the stitches to match the knitting stitches. In other words, if the yarn is not thick enough to cover the background as you work from one knitted stitch to the next, use a thicker yarn or take several strands together.

Satin stitch has been used in samples 13, 35 and 44.

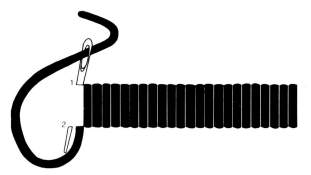

Stem stitch

This stitch can be mirrored to suit the knitting. Work from left to right, or from bottom to top. Bring needle down at 1 and up at 2. In the illustration, point 2 is higher than point 1 from the stitch before. If the stitch was following rows, point 2 could be on the row above 1. For a thinner effect, stay on the same row all the time, bringing the needle up at the point where it went down on the previous stitch. To mirror backstitch, make point 2 lower than point 1 or, in the thin version, bring the needle up under the yarn instead of over it. Two mirrored lines close together look effective.

Stem stitch was used in samples 8, 14, 30, 32 and 43.

Chain stitch

One interesting aspect of this stitch is that it can also be made using a crochet hook; another one is that it can be threaded in the same ways as running stitch and backstitch. Work from right to left, or from top to bottom. Start the chain by bringing the needle up at 1. Insert it in the same place and bring it up again at 2. Carry the embroidery yarn under the needle before pulling the needle through. Point 2 becomes point 1 of next stitch. To end the chain, take the needle down at 3 to secure the last loop of yarn.

Chain stitch has been used in samples 9, 38 and 41.

Zigzag chain stitch

This is just like chain stitch, except that points 1 and 2 move from side to side. In embroidered knitting, you simply place them on different rows or stitch lines.

Zigzag chain stitch has been used in sample 16.

Detached chain stitch

This is another variation of chain stitch, which is like the first and last stitch of a long chain, all in one. Bring needle up at 1, down again at 1 and up at 2. Carry the embroidery yarn under the needle before pulling the needle through. Insert yarn at 3 to secure the loop of yarn, and bring up at 4. Point 4 is point 1 in next stitch.

Detached chain stitch has been used in sample 6.

Backstitch

Of all the unbroken lines that can be obtained in embroidery, backstitch is the thinnest. The straight lines of the stitches follow each other without interruption or overlap. On the wrong side, it is exactly like stem stitch done over a single line. Work from right to left, or from top to bottom. Bring needle up at 1, down at 2, and up again at 3. Point 3 is point 1 in next stitch.

Backstitch was used in samples 15, 24, 37 and 48.

Threaded backstitch

Like running stitch, backstitch can be threaded with the same yarn or with a contrasting one. Also as in running stitch, raised lines in the knitting (or a different embroidery stitch) can be used as a foundation instead of backstitch. Work can progress from left to right, as in the illustration, or from right to left. This gives a mirrored image of the way in which the loops cross. The loops can also, just as easily, be made to cross above the foundation, rather than below.

Threaded backstitch was used in samples 23 and 27.

Zigzag backstitch

This is like backstitch, but worked over two parallel lines. The two stitches can easily be combined. Bring needle up at 1, down at 2, up at 3, down at 1 and up at 4. Work from right to left, keeping the needle horizontal. Two lines can be worked on top of each other, staggering the points the needle goes through.

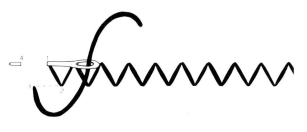

If the two lines are in the same yarn, the result is like cross stitch. If they are in contrast yarns, the two zigzags can be clearly identified.

Zigzag backstitch was used in samples 20, 33, 39 and 47.

Four-sided stitch

This stitch can be used to work individual squares, or the long lines shown in the illustration. The squares can easily be turned into rectangles, by elongating them in either direction. Work from right to left. The needle goes twice into each point. Bring it up at 1, down at 2, up at 3, down at 1, up at 4, down at 2, up at 3, down at 4. Point 3 becomes point 1 of next stitch, and point 4 becomes point 2.

Four-sided stitch was used in samples 13, 26 and 46.

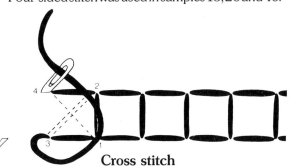

Cross stitch

This can be worked in either direction. To work from left to right, bring needle up at 1, down at 2, up at 3 and down at 4. If the crosses are worked together, point 4 becomes point 2 in the next stitch, and point 1 becomes point 3. To work from right to left, proceed in the same way. In the next stitch, point 3 becomes point 1, and point 2 becomes point 4.

Cross stitch has been used in samples 5, 26 and 45.

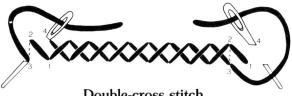

Double-cross stitch

On the wrong side, this little trellis looks like two parallel rows of backstitch. Work from left to right. Bring needle up at 1, down at 2, up at 3, down at 4 and

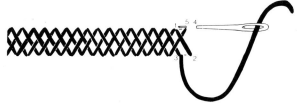

up at 5. Point 5 is point 1 of next stitch.

Double-cross stitch has been used in sample 20.

Chevron stitch

This looks rather like zigzag backstitch combined with two lines of running stitch, but is done in one single go. Starting on the bottom line, bring needle down at 1, up at 2, down at 3 and up at 1. Move to the top line and go down at 4, up at 5, down at 6 and up at 4. Move to the bottom line again.

Chevron stitch has been used in samples 7 and 28.

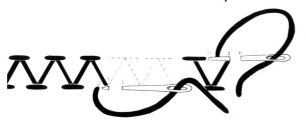

Cable hemstitch

This is usually worked around free strands but can be adapted to other knitting situations. Bring needle up at 1, down at 2, up at 3, down at 4, up at 5, down at 6, up at 7, down at 8 and up at 9. Point 9 becomes point 1 in next stitch. In the illustration, the gaps between the stitches have been left to make room for point numbers. And this is also what the stitch looks like when it is worked around loose strands – it has a gathering effect and gaps appear. In fact, points 1, 3, 4 and 6 are the same point. Points 2, 5, 7 and 8 are also the same point.

Cable hemstitch has been used in sample 22.

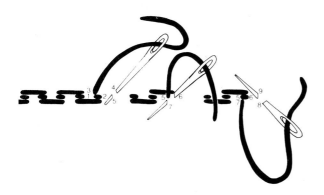

Honeycomb stitch

This is a stitch used to gather fabric in smocking. In conventional embroidery, the fabric would need to be prepared by many tacking rows – to set the gathers. In embroidered knitting, the gathers are set by working a 'knit one, purl several' pattern. The purl stitches curl out at the sides, raising the lines with the single knit stitch. To make embroidering easier, thread a fine contrast through the knit stitches of the row under the knitting needle from time to time. Work 'one stitch above' or 'three stitches below tacking'.

Only the knit stitch is caught by the needle. Work from left to right. Starting on the lower row, bring needle up at 1, down at 2, up at 3 (right under 1), down at 4 (right under 2), up at 5, down at 6, up at 7 (right above 5), down at 8 (right above 6) and up at 9. Point 9 becomes point 1 of next stitch.

Honeycomb stitch has been used in sample 28.

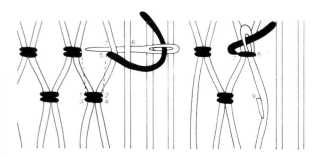

Vandyke stitch

This is similar to honeycomb stitch, but the strands between the two lines are visible, and it is worked from right to left. Coming from the top row, bring needle down at 1, up at 2, down at 1 again, up at 2 again, down at 3 on the top row, up at 4, down at 3 again, up at 4 again, down at 5 on the bottom row – which will be point 1 of next stitch.

Vandyke stitch has been used in sample 29.

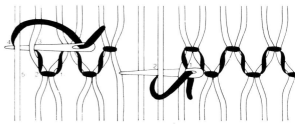

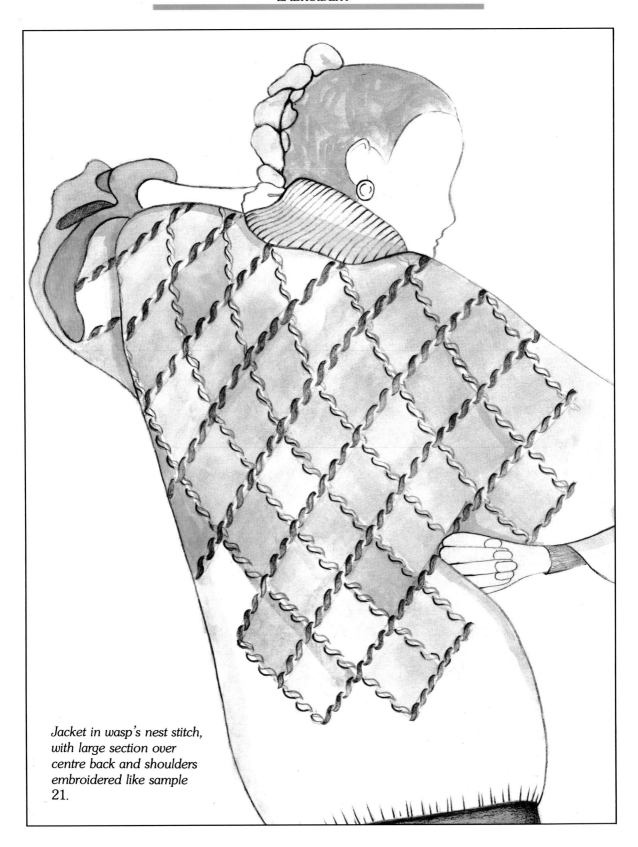

Jacket in wasp's nest stitch, with large section over centre back and shoulders embroidered like sample 21.

5 PROJECT IDEAS

One of the nicest things about embroidered knitting is that you can get on with it straightaway. If you have been smitten with the bug and can't wait to knit a sweater to give it a try, don't worry. If you are not a knitter, don't worry either. Just take a sweater you already have or, if you can't find a suitable one at home, go and buy one. It doesn't need to be hand knitted. Any kind of knitting, so long as it has a suitable pattern, can be embroidered. Six samples in Part Two are machine knitted, and half the sweaters in the photographs are factory made.

If the sweater you are starting on has a pattern that can be highlighted, work on that – the **Embroidery** section can help you decide what to do with it. If it is in plain stocking stitch, stress the seams (as in samples 43 to 48), or build up something around the borders (as in samples 37 to 42).

Sweaters are not, by any means, the only things that can be embroidered. There are coats, dresses, scarves, hats, shawls, gloves and socks. And there are also rugs, bags, cushion covers, bedspreads and wallhangings.

Whether you knit something especially or not, you can use the embroidery all over, or only on one or two places – as shown in the illustrations. You can also start by embroidering a strategically placed band, and then carry on adding to it if you enjoy the experience.

If you don't like the way something is turning out, or if you suddenly discover that the sky blue should have been peacock blue and the sorbet orange should have been tangerine, it won't take you long to put matters right. This is not like knitting a multi-coloured project,

where to unpick ten stitches you have to unravel everything. If something does not please you, simply unpick that bit and do it again. If there is too much navy, add a touch of vivid yellow. If the purple is too vibrant, add some pale dull green. If chain stitch is too fussy, use backstitch instead.

Certain kinds of embroidery involve long stitches that might easily get caught. Don't use them for knitwear. Or, if you do, restrict them to the less risky areas – such as the top half of sweaters or coats. Thick, heavy, matt, and especially slubby or knobbly yarns, are less prone to snag if they get caught.

How much yarn will you need? If you know how many metres/yards there are in a ball, cut off five of them. Cut them again into manageable lengths, and see how much you can embroider with them. Work out what fraction of the overall embroidery that is. If it is a twentieth, you will need 100 metres/yards. If it is a tenth, you will need 50. And if it is a fiftieth, you will need 250. In other words, you multiply whatever fraction it is by five.

This kind of reckoning could also be done with only one or two metres/yards, but it would be less accurate.

If the ball band doesn't give the necessary information, ask at the shop where you bought the yarn. The manufacturer's shade card might tell, even if the band does not. If someone at the shop can't help, or if you are using leftover yarn bought some time ago, either unwind and measure a ball yourself, or weigh 10g($\frac{1}{2}$oz) as accurately as you can, and then measure that.

Have fun!

Sweater in zigzag-check stitch, with two bands of embroidery around body and single motif over cuff as in Sample 13. Shoulder, cuff and waistband seams as in Sample 44.

This hazelnut brown jacket, hand knitted in a mottled, chunky Shetland-type wool, had seen three winters before any embroidery was applied to it. The knitted pattern produces a chequerboard arrangement of diamonds in double moss stitch (see Sample 9). This stitch, plus a combination of knit centres for the diamonds, and a purl background, resulted in a fabric with no curl, which was ideally suited to the straight lines of the jacket – even if the diamonds were not especially obvious.

The embroidery simply outlines the diamonds with running stitch. It moves over the surface of the knitting, just catching the pips of the purl stitches. At the top and bottom, however, the needle had to be taken through to the wrong side, to anchor the yarn before changing direction. Three dark-to-light shades of tapestry wool were chosen for each line of diamonds. Colours change upwards from yellowy apricot to deep rose, and from greenish kingfisher to bright sky blue.

Sweater in stocking stitch, with sailor collar and cuffs knitted and embroidered like sample 4.

Right: *This blue cotton jumper is a very good example of a sweater specifically designed for embroidery. Sample 17 was adapted to three brightly contrasting shades and a single, somewhat different border was used. Because the project was to be used for knitwear, the risk of snagging had to be minimized. First, zigzag backstitch was chosen in preference to the whipped running stitch of the original. This makes the yarn enter the eyelets at a different angle, but the result is more stable if a strand is pulled. Second, the eyelets were worked much closer together. Finally, the embroidery was restricted to a narrow strip at the front and the short sleeves.*

The front inset was worked separately so that the embroidery could be anchored at the side edges and then hidden in a seam. But, to ensure that the seam was tidy and flat, it was essential to knit the body in a pattern that didn't curl, and so neatly that the edges could be simply stitched on top of the embroidered piece, without being folded under. Because of this, the body was worked in moss stitch, with increases at centre back (and at centre front before the parting of the sides). A few short rows above the waistband complemented the increases and ensured that the front V formed of its own accord once the front was divided, that the shoulders sloped down without any further shaping, and that the sleeves continued the shoulder slope – a rather good move to eliminate excessive bulk under the arm.

Blouse in k1, p4 rib, with cuffs like Sample 28. Shorter versions of the smocking pattern on stand-up collar and waistband. The ruffles form naturally at the edge of the embroidery.

This Stefanel jumper in a wool, acrylic and alpaca blend was made in Italy. With its precise styling and its neat arrangement of small cables around neckline and waist, it is the most expensive of the four sweaters that have come from shops – and it shows. The seams are beautifully worked, the cables are placed so that they flow over the seams without visible interruption, the detailing is immaculate and the yarn is soft and warm. So simple and yet so skilful.

The only thing to do was to emphasize what was already there, by making the cables more clearly visible. To this end, the spaces in between cables were embroidered in three shades of real Shetland wool. The technique was as easy and as simple as the sweater: running stitch caught the top loop of each fourth purl stitch, just as in Sample 36.

Jacket in small mock-cable stitch, with sections embroidered like Sample 31.

The embroidery on this vivid orange sweater is an afterthought. The sweater had been hand knitted from the bottom up, with increases at the sides for the sleeves and then carefully positioned increases and short rows to make the sleeves follow the body line, rather like classic inset sleeves. The chevron made by the short rows running down the shoulder and sleeve line had been emphasized with welting, but because of the fuzziness of the pure mohair yarn, the pattern made by the welts didn't show up much. Chain stitching the grooves with violet-coloured chenille (as in Sample 41 but with longer stitches) soon remedied this by highlighting the chevrons.

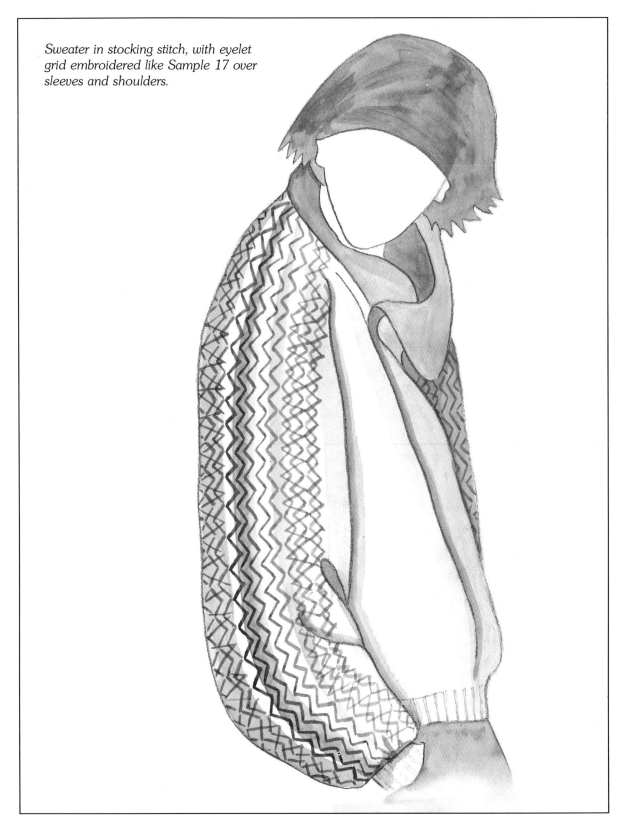

Sweater in stocking stitch, with eyelet grid embroidered like Sample 17 over sleeves and shoulders.

This unusually patterned sweater is from Solo, a British chain of boutiques specializing in quality and design at affordable prices. It is a well-made piece, bright, cheerful and fashionably styled. The inset sleeves and the front button band suggested an embroidered sort of yoke, moving upwards from the end of the band to not far below the shoulders. The distinctive pattern clearly indicated what stitches ought to be used: zigzag backstitch across the knitted zigzags, and ordinary backstitch on the edges of each narrow panel. The clear emerald green of the wool and acrylic yarn inspired the final choice: bold, summery colours and a crinkly cotton yarn.

PART TWO
SAMPLES
MOSS STITCH

Moss stitch is like a knitting equivalent of graph paper. With its raised chequerboard of knit and purl stitches, it is just the perfect base for several kinds of geometric embroidery – most especially pattern darning and other variations of running stitch. Because it never curls, it is also ideal for borders or for knitting projects that need to hang perfectly straight.

In France, Italy and Spain, moss stitch is known as 'rice stitch'. Looking at the neatly arranged grains made by the purl stitches, it is not difficult to see why.

A moss-stitch grid runs in two main directions: vertical and diagonal. Either of them can be picked up by working along the clean, low lines between purl stitches, or by burrowing under the purl stitches.

Horizontal lines are rather unclear. If a horizontal emphasis is essential, knit the piece from side to side and follow a vertical line. Alternatively, outline the stepped knit or purl stitches of two consecutive rows. This can be done, for example, with a zigzagging line, or with whipped running stitch.

It is easier to work moss stitch over an odd number of stitches, than over an even number. In the first instance, all the rows are alike:

> *k1, p1, repeat from *, end k1

With an even number of stitches, there is a second row:

> *p1, k1, repeat from *, end p1

The only difference is the order of the stitches. With an odd number you can start all your rows automatically, without checking whether to do a knit or a purl first.

The size of the embroidery designs in all the samples that follow can easily be adapted to suit different yarns, tensions and applications.

SAMPLE 1

● ● ● KNITTING ● ● ●
Moss stitch in yarn 43.

● ● ● EMBROIDERY ● ● ●
Running stitch in the same yarn (two strands).

The yarn used for knitting this sample has quite a high gloss. Added to its bright colour, this gives very good contrasts between light and shadow. The resulting fabric is three-dimensional and very lively.

The same yarn was chosen for the embroidery, in two neutral shades this time. By using one shade for the vertical lines and the other for diagonals, the

structure of the embroidery is made clear, and depth is gained.

Embroider first the diagonals, along the knit lines. Bring the needle up and down through the fabric every two stitches. Repeat on every fourth diagonal, reversing the order in which the needle is brought up and down.

Embroider every fourth vertical knit line also, bringing the needle down and up to catch every fourth row – always the one across the embroidered diagonals – to produce a basket-weave effect. If using two strands of yarn for the embroidery, as in the example, try to keep them untwisted and at a similar tension.

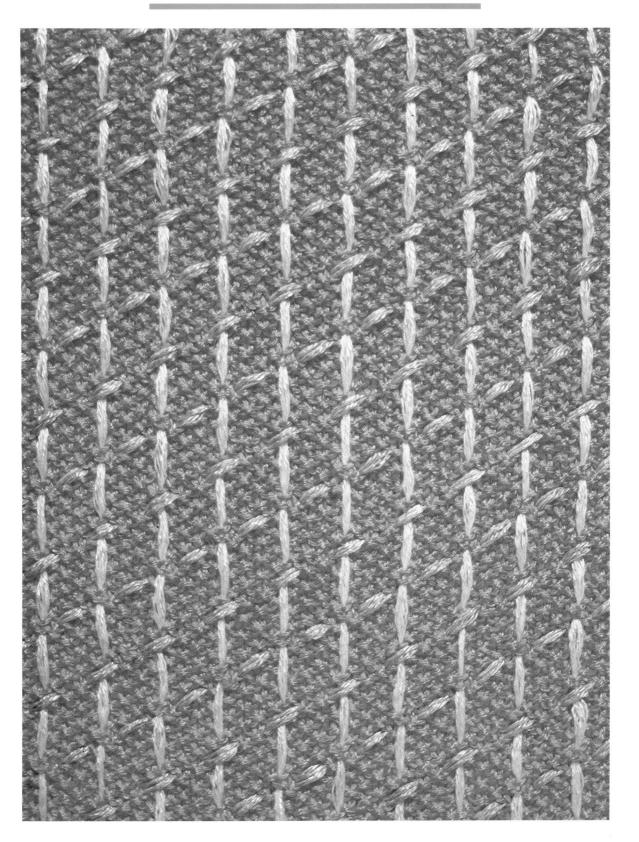

SAMPLE 2

● ● ●KNITTING● ● ●

Moss stitch in yarn 45.

● ● ● EMBROIDERY● ● ●

Threaded running stitch in yarn 49 (two strands).

This interesting pattern requires a certain amount of attention. Before starting to work, plot all the high and low chevron points with safety pins or outline the chevrons with rows of tacking. These can be in a fine, smooth yarn, or in ordinary sewing cotton if the knitting is thin enough.

If you like the concept of the embroidery, but would prefer a simpler version of it, try burrowing under the purl stitches with an ordinary running stitch, rather than moving snake-fashion from one stitch to the next. Or use threaded running stitch, like the sample, but make diagonal bands rather than chevrons.

The sample is knitted at a very loose tension because of the weight of the glossy ribbon yarn. The sparkling embroidery yarn was chosen because it looked stunning next to the ribbon, and because it was so light that it would add no real weight to the knitting. The ribbon was kept as untwisted as possible during knitting, to make sure that the purl stitches were well shaped, and had the special depth that only untwisted ribbon gives.

Work to and fro, along diagonals, in threaded running stitch. You can see in the chart that breaks occur at certain points. When this happens, bring the needle down into the knit stitch past the last purl stitch. Anchor and trim the yarn. Rejoin as indicated in the chart. Work the next diagonal in the same direction as the last one.

Notice that the way in which the chevrons are embroidered has been alternated. Some are right handed, and some are left handed.

On the wrong side, you can only see yarn joins where there is a change of direction. If diagonal bands were worked instead of chevrons, and long lengths of yarn were used, the embroidery would not show on the wrong side.

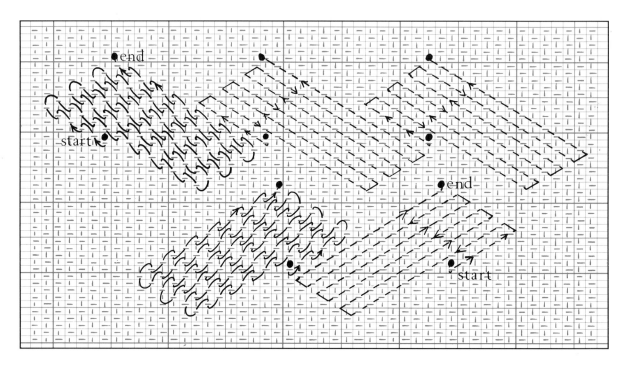

SAMPLE 3

● ● ●KNITTING ● ● ●

Moss stitch in yarn 4 (double knitting).

● ● ●EMBROIDERY ● ● ●

Offset running stitch in four light-to-dark shades of yarn 4 (tapestry wool).

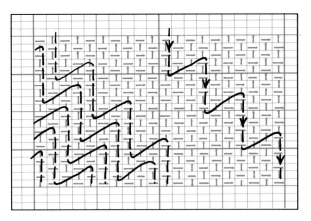

The embroidery pattern in this sample, based in the old huckaback embroidery, is very easy to execute. Once the first row is set, the rest become quite automatic.

All rows move diagonally, from top left to bottom right. Start along a line that roughly divides the area to be embroidered into two. Set the first row and, one by one, work all the rows below this one. When there are no rows left, turn the knitting and finish the embroidery in exactly the same way. The order of the shading will be reversed, but the working method will not be altered.

To set the first row, and to work all the other rows:

> from top left – *push needle under four purl stitches from the first vertical line; pull yarn through; following the diagonal line made by the knit stitches, move to the third vertical purl line to the right, and repeat from *

To prevent the yarn from pulling the top purl stitch out of shape, keep the stitch in place with your left thumb-nail.

In the example, the shade of the embroidery yarn changes from one row to the next. It goes from natural to medium-brown in four stages, and then straight to natural again. This makes the embroidery far more intriguing and dynamic than it would otherwise have been.

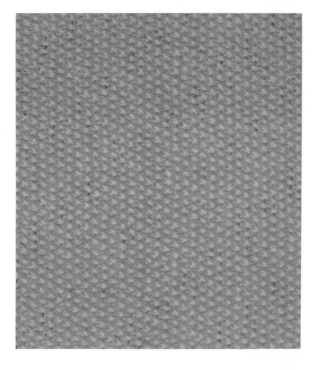

The embroidery doesn't show on the wrong side.

SAMPLE 4

●●●KNITTING●●●
Moss stitch in yarn 18 (two strands).

●●● EMBROIDERY●●●
Offset running stitch in yarns 45 and 46.

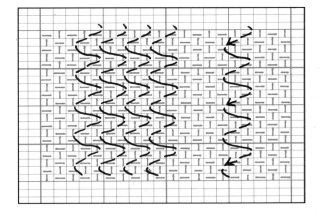

The mohair used in this sample is very fine so two strands were worked together for a chunkier result. The embroidery follows a very similar approach to that of sample 3. Work it in narrow vertical lines, weaving the yarn diagonally this time.

Dark glossy ribbon was chosen because it offered such a stark contrast with the fuzziness of the mohair. The off-white ribbon, with its mother-of-pearl sparkle, provides additional colour and texture contrast. It also helps to highlight the structure of the embroidery pattern. It was faster to work with than the grey ribbon because there was no need to keep it untwisted as it went in and out of the stitches. The special way in which the grey ribbon narrows as it approaches the stitches is, however, worth every extra minute fiddling.

To work each line of embroidery:

> from top left – *following a diagonal line, push needle under three purl stitches, from right to left; pull yarn; move across to the right again, and repeat from * starting two purl bumps below the first one

To start the next vertical stripe, move two stitches to the right of where you started the first line. In other words, move to the next purl stitch on the starting row.

The embroidery doesn't show on the wrong side.

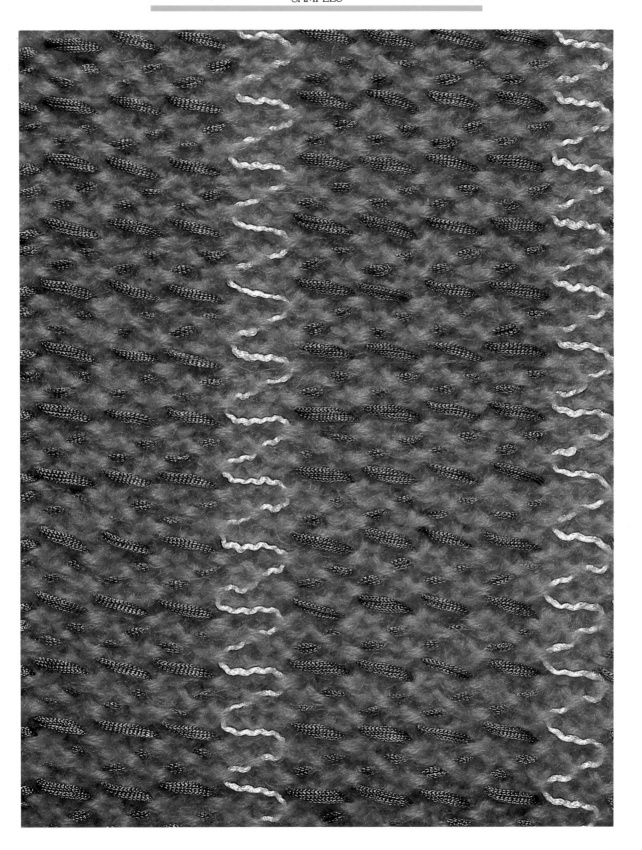

STRIPES

Horizontal stripes come in many guises. With only one exception (sample 10), the examples that follow have all been knitted in a single colour. With the same exception, the embroidery has been added to stress the horizontal emphasis of the knitting.

Use stripes individually or all over. Make them in the stitches suggested or search for new ones. Many patterns can be turned into stripes and, if the ideal can't be found, new ones can always be adapted or invented.

SAMPLE 5

●●●KNITTING●●●
Stocking stitch with moss stitch rows, in yarn 40 (two strands).

●●●EMBROIDERY●●●
Cross stitch in yarn 42.

Two strands of fine, deep burgundy chenille were knitted together for this sample. After 14 rows of stocking stitch, two rows of moss stitch were introduced (see page 42). Because chenille rather blurs the outline of the stitches, it turns moss stitch into neat lines of raised dashes – rather as if it was trying to get to the essence of the stitch.

The knitting, thanks to the chenille, is rich and sumptuous, with a very special kind of velvety sheen. If a surface could be matt and lustrous at the same time, this would be it.

The embroidery yarn was chosen to reflect the dual quality of the chenille. One of its plies is glossy, the other matt. Because of its slight slubbiness and loose twist, it gives height to the cross stitches, while blurring their outline – rather like the chenille blurs the knitted stitches.

The double line of cross stitch reflects the double line of moss stitch. It is worked as one single row. The position of every other stitch goes up one row, but otherwise work progresses as for ordinary cross stitch.

Work each cross to cover a knit stitch.

To make sure that you can embroider in straight lines without any difficulties, thread contrasts while you are knitting – as explained on page 29.

SAMPLE 6

●●●KNITTING●●●
Welting in yarn 30.

●●●EMBROIDERY●●●
Detached chain stitch in yarn 26.

Stocking-stitch welting is nothing more than stocking stitch, showing now the knit side, now the purl side. Because of the natural curl of the fabric, the purl bands receive a dramatic lift, while the knit bands make deep furrows.

Welting requires much yarn and does not progress very quickly, because of the many ins and outs, but it is a wonderful fabric. Its lively concertina movement can be used to great effect in many design situations.

The knit and purl bands can be made as wide or as narrow as the yarn or situation require. They can be of similar width, or one can be wider than the other. In the sample, the following sequence was used:

```
row 1 – purl
row 2 – knit
row 3 – purl
row 4 – knit
row 5 – purl
```

These five rows were repeated over and over.

To establish the sequence that suits you best, work a small sample in stocking stitch (knit one row, purl one row). When the first band seems wide enough, work a row like the one last done. It doesn't matter whether it is a knit or a purl row. Either way it will change the side of the fabric you see. When the second band looks wide enough, knit again a row like the one last done. Because of the concertina effect, the bands usually need to be wider than one thinks.

Welting was chosen in this case because it shows so well the purl side of stocking stitch and, therefore, was perfect for the textured knitting yarn.

The embroidery yarn, so smooth and even, provides a good contrast. The delicacy of its many shades and the way in which these blend into each other, add a gentle touch to a bold piece of knitting.

Detached chain stitches were worked with this yarn, leaving three knitted stitches in between. They were staggered from one band to the next. Each one starts and ends one row away from the change-of-pattern line. This makes it very easy to make them all the same size.

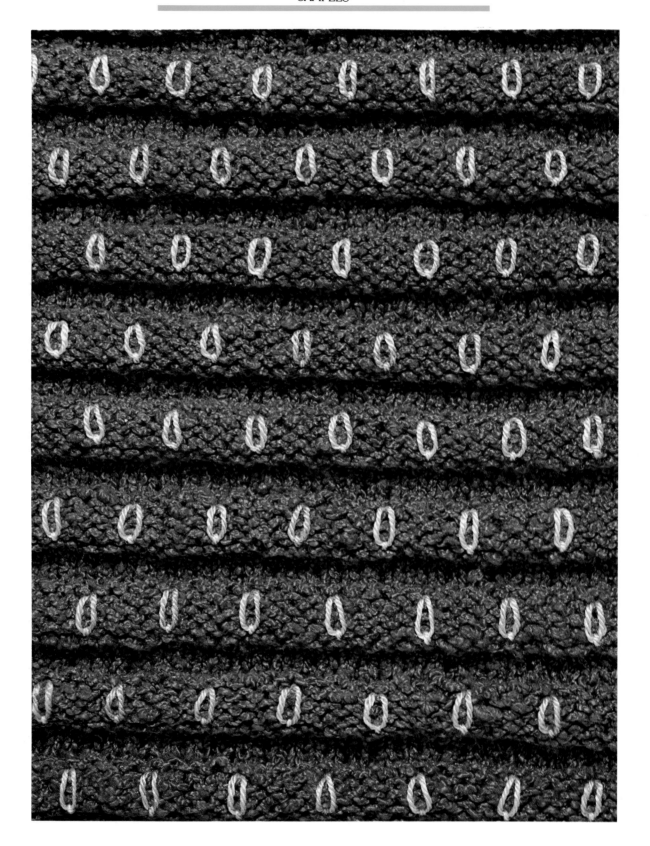

SAMPLE 7

●●●KNITTING●●●

Stocking stitch with dotted purl stitches, in yarn 5.

●●●EMBROIDERY●●●

Chevron stitch in yarn 35.

On this occasion, it is not so much the embroidery emphasizing the knitting, as the knitting being planned with a particular embroidery stitch in mind. The idea was to have a very plain fabric on which to embroider lines of chevron stitch that picked up the shades of some of the flecks in the knitting yarn.

If the fabric had been pure stocking stitch, to work the chevron lines would have involved much counting and agonizing. This was avoided simply by placing a few purl stitches in strategic points. These are easy to work, give the exact position of the chevron points, and underline the short strands of the embroidery pattern.

Along a knit row, every fourth stitch was purled:

> *k3, p1, repeat from *

A second, staggered line was knitted four rows later:

> k1, p1, *k3, p1, repeat from *, end k1

This arrangement was repeated on the following eighth and twelfth rows.

The embroidery simply follows the purl stitches. Point 1 is the centre of the stitch above a first-row purl stitch. Points 2 and 3 are at the sides of this stitch. Point 4 is the centre of the stitch below a fourth-row purl stitch. Points 5 and 6 are at the sides of this stitch.

SAMPLE 8

● ● ●KNITTING● ● ●

Purl side of stocking stitch, with knit rows, in yarn 15.

● ● ●EMBROIDERY● ● ●

Stem stitch in yarn 2 (four strands).

As in sample 6, the purl side of stocking stitch was a good option for the chosen knitting yarn. In this case, the slubs were better displayed, and the many bright colours better blended, on the purl side than on the knit side.

To make the stocking stitch curl less than it normally does, pairs of knit grooves were introduced from time to time. The rows were arranged as follows:

row 1 – purl
row 2 – knit
row 3 – purl
row 4 – knit
row 5 – purl
rows 6 to 10 – knit

The knit grooves were embroidered in stem stitch, using a Shetland mixture that subtly picks up most of the colours in the knitting yarn. Four strands were worked together to make a thick rope that would fill the groove. Points 1 and 2 were kept at different levels within the groove to give extra twist to the stem-stitch rope.

The second row of stem stitch was made to mirror the first one, by bringing the needle up on the other side of the yarn. The two ropes became, in this way, a single design unit.

Despite its great thickness, the embroidery hardly raises above the knitting, because it sinks into the knit grooves.

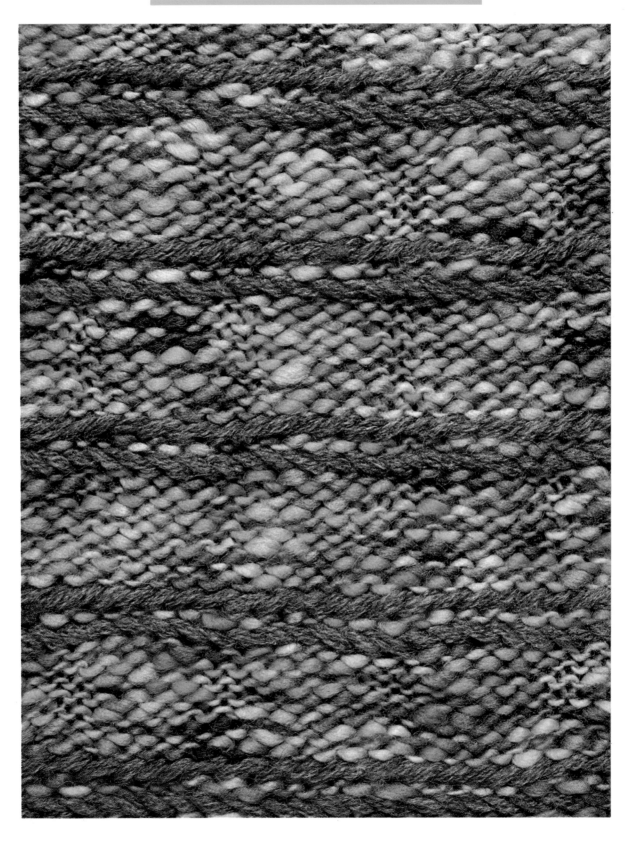

SAMPLE 9

●●●KNITTING●●●
Textured bands in yarn 9.

●●●EMBROIDERY●●●
Chain stitch in yarn 21, and running stitch in yarn 41.

Because it is unplied and has such a light twist, the knitting yarn chosen for this sample shows individual fibres more clearly than most other yarns. The two embroidery yarns, in their own very different fashions, show individual fibres in even greater clarity.

The thick chenille displays a deep pile of cut fibres. It was kept fairly untwisted while embroidering, but the pile does not always lie in the same direction. The yarn then catches the light in different ways, and this makes some spots look much brighter than others.

The brushed lustre wool shows its own fibres in all their splendour, and the delicate changes in colour of this yarn reflect rather well, in a much larger scale, the apparent colour changes in the chenille.

After working the thin lines of chain stitch, the wool was thoroughly re-brushed. Take great care not to upset the other yarns when doing this. If the edge of an ordinary brush doesn't prove suitable, try a brand new and extra hard toothbrush.

In the sample, the pattern lines are divided by four rows of stocking stitch. This number can easily be altered, but always have an even number of rows. After the last (purl) row of stocking stitch, start the pattern stripe:

```
rows 1 to 3 – knit
rows 4 to 6 – purl
```

Continue in double moss stitch for an even number of rows (10 in sample). On an even number of stitches, double moss stitch is worked as follows:

```
rows 1 and 2 – *k1, p1, repeat from *
rows 3 and 4 – *p1, k1, repeat from *
```

Repeat the previous sequence of three knit and three purl rows. This ends the pattern band. Add the desired length of stocking stitch before working the next band, or use just one band all by itself.

Double moss stitch is ideal for running-stitch embroidery. Of each pair of look-alike rows, embroider the top one. Bring the needle down and up to leave the knit stitches in view and the purl stitches hiding. Don't have more than three stitches on the needle when you pull the yarn – the running stitches will be too tight and uneven otherwise. Keep the tension fairly loose so that the stitches show well, and even it out before moving on to the next needleful.

One line of chain stitch was worked along each one of the grooves created by the three knit and three purl rows. One stitch was placed over each knitted stitch. The tension was kept loose, so that the chain would fill the whole width of the groove.

SAMPLE 10

●●●KNITTING●●●
Garter stitch in yarn 27.

●●●EMBROIDERY●●●
Running stitch in the same yarn.

Unlike the other samples in this group, this one was knitted in colour stripes, rather than texture stripes. Also, unlike the others, the embroidery was used to create checks out of the stripes, rather than to emphasize the horizontal patterning.

Neither the knitting, nor the embroidery, could be simpler. Garter stitch (knit all rows) and running stitch are the most elementary of stitches. Garter stitch makes a fabric that doesn't curl, but is normally rather slow in growing. In this case it has to be knitted quite loosely to keep the final result supple and so it grows much faster. The tendency to spread of all slack knitting is kept in check by the embroidery.

Making the knitting more stable through the embroidery was important in this case. The yarn chosen has little resilience. It stretches easily, but it recovers its original size and shape with difficulty.

Many kinds of stripes and checks can be worked. The sample is based on equally-sized horizontal and vertical bands, following a similar colour sequence: soft green, apricot and muddy mauve.

Each knitted colour band has an even number of rows. In garter stitch, colour changes show a broken line on one side. These can be used to advantage in some situations, but in this case they were best avoided, so they had to be kept all on the same side of the work.

Before embroidering, block the knitting, making sure it is well stretched, then measure the depth of a stripe. Lay the tape measure along a row and count how many stitches are needed to make a square. In the sample, there were 12 rows in a stripe – showing as six raised lines. Four and a half stitches were enough to create a square. However, two embroidery lines run along each stitch, so nine embroidery rows were required for each square.

Work the running stitches as shown in the diagram. Each horizontal raised line has high and low points. On the first row of running stitches, catch the high points of every other horizontal line. On the second row, catch the low points of the lines you missed on the first row. Repeat these two rows.

The final result is rather like woven cloth on the right side.

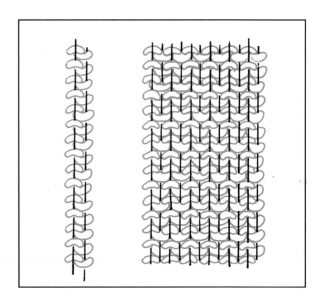

On the wrong side, only the knitted stripes show.

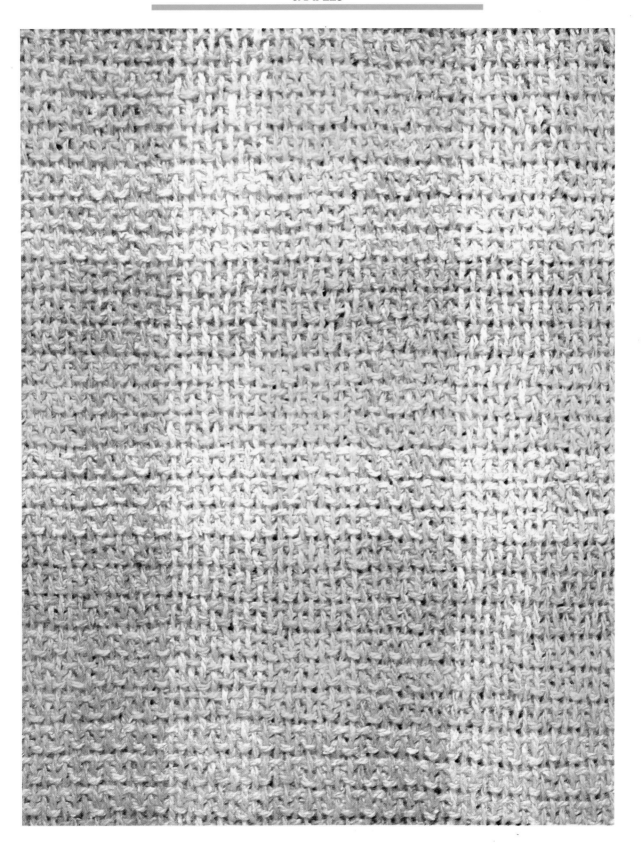

KNIT-AND-PURL PATTERNS

This group covers combinations of knit and purl stitches that give an all-over pattern, but put no special emphasis on horizontal, vertical or diagonal lines.

To belong to this group, a pattern must be easily recognizable. Stitches with very small units, for example, are not included in this group because they require a different kind of approach. Moss stitch, a good example of small-unit pattern, has been covered in the first group of samples.

When a pattern has a very strong image, the embroidery should reinforce it. Clear, strong statements are an essential part of good design. Many knit-and-purl combinations, however, can be interpreted in different ways. It is up to you to choose one of them and make your statement. For example, you can give a definite direction to a pattern that doesn't have one, or you can discover and isolate motifs that didn't seem to be there.

SAMPLE 11

● ● ● KNITTING ● ● ●

Short columns of knit stitches on a purl background, in yarn 38.

● ● ● EMBROIDERY ● ● ●

Threaded running stitch in yarn 9 (two strands).

The very thick cotton chosen to knit this sample gives very clear stitches. Its neutral colour is enhanced by the two embroidery shades. The light terracotta adds warmth. The very deep blue balances this warmth with its own coolness, while giving a new glow to the knitting yarn.

The pattern of the knitting is very straightforward. Columns of single knit stitches are kept apart by an odd number of purl stitches (five in the sample). After a few rows (six in the sample), the columns are staggered.

Instructions for the sample, on a multiple of six stitches plus five stitches, read:

rows 1, 3, 5 (right side) – p5, *k1, p5, repeat from *
rows 2, 4, 6 – k5, *p1, k5, repeat from *
rows 7, 9, 11 – p2, k1, *p5, k1, repeat from *, end p2
rows 8, 10, 12 – k2, p1, *k5, p1, repeat from *, end k2

The knit columns stand out of their own accord from the purl background. Threaded running stitch was chosen to stress this natural tendency – further stressed by embroidery yarns which are darker than the knitting yarn. The embroidery is worked by moving the needle in and out of each knit stitch. When a column is finished, take the yarn onto the next. If the columns are spaced a long way from each other, anchor, trim and re-join the yarn instead.

The embroidery colours are arranged along diagonals. This gives one of many possible interpretations of the knitting pattern. Merely by changing the colour arrangement, the pattern could yield vertical or horizontal lines, diamonds, vertical or horizontal zigzags, and others.

SAMPLE 12

●●●KNITTING●●●
Short columns of garter stitch on a stocking stitch background in yarn 10.

●●●EMBROIDERY●●●
Running stitch in yarn 12.

odd-numbered rows (right side) – knit
rows 2, 4, 6, 8 – p7, *k1, p7, repeat from *
rows 10, 12, 14, 16 – p3, k1, *p7, k1, repeat from *, p3.

This knitting pattern is very much like the one used for sample 11, but seen from the other side. There are seven stitches instead of five between columns, and these are staggered every eight rows instead of every six; the concept, however, is very similar.

Where samples 11 and 12 differ is in the way of working the columns. On a knit background, columns of purl stitches would sink and half disappear from sight. Columns of garter stitch, on the other hand, rise high above the knit background. Every two rows of garter stitch make a bumpy loop. A line of these loops makes an ideal channel for surface embroidery.

The number of stitches and rows can be varied at will, but instructions for the sample, on a multiple of eight stitches plus seven stitches, read:

The wool roving used for the embroidery blends very well with the knitted lopi wool, because they both display individual fibres in a similar fashion. The space-dyeing of the roving, with its clear blues turning to muddy browns, gives movement to the exceptionally simple embroidery.

Other kinds of embroidery could be used to bring out the same patterns mentioned for sample 11, but a different embroidery yarn would be required. The roving has so much character, and makes such an impact, that it is best to use it very simply. Burrowing under the garter stitch in straight, vertical lines, was the obvious answer.

SAMPLE 13

●●●KNITTING●●●
Zigzag check in yarn 1 (machine knitted).

●●●EMBROIDERY●●●
Satin stitch and four-sided stitch in yarn 28.

The knitting pattern in this sample makes a very interesting fabric which does not curl, because the knit and purl stitches are well balanced.

The pattern is very dynamic, and is best described as a distorted chequerboard. Groups of four purl and four knit stitches alternate throughout. Sometimes they keep vertical sides for four rows. Sometimes they travel one stitch towards the right on each row for five rows. And sometimes they travel one stitch towards the left on each row for five rows. Before a change takes place, there is always a plain row. This is knitted if worked with the right side facing, purled if worked with the wrong side facing.

Instructions on a multiple of eight stitches read:

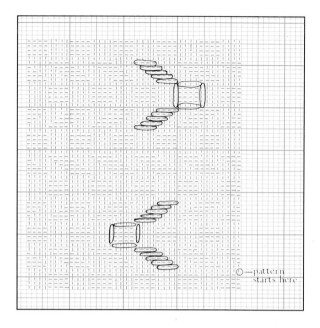

○—pattern
starts here

row 1 (right side) – knit
row 2 – *k4, p4, repeat from *
row 3 – p1, *k4, p4, repeat from *, end last repeat p3
row 4 – k2, *p4, k4, repeat from *, end last repeat k2
row 5 – p3, *k4, p4, repeat from *, end last repeat p1
row 6 – *p4, k4, repeat from *
row 7 – knit
row 8 to 11 – *k4, p4, repeat from *
row 12 – purl
row 13 – *p4, k4, repeat from *
row 14 – k1, *p4, k4, repeat from *, end last repeat k3
row 15 – p2, *k4, p4, repeat from *, end last repeat p2
row 16 – k3, *p4, k4, repeat from *, end last repeat k1
row 17 – *k4, p4, repeat from *
row 18 – purl
rows 19 to 22 – *p4, k4, repeat from *

The embroidery reveals the three ways in which the stitches travel, by combining three stitch blocks into single motifs. Having some lines of motifs pointing to the right and others to the left, added to the illusion of flying conveyed by the motifs, highlights the dynamic character of the pattern.

A very special silk was chosen for the embroidery. Its ever-changing, luminous colours are yet another way of bringing movement into the sample. The silk is just of the right thickness to cover a complete knitting row. This is used to advantage in the satin stitch worked on the wings of the motifs. Satin stitch, in this case, is easiest to work from the bottom up, rather than sideways. The knitted rows and stitches are then the right way up, and can be clearly identified when trying to see where to bring the needle up or down.

Make the satin stitch travel diagonally, following the purl stitches that you are covering. Bring the needle up from the first knit stitch at one side of the panel, and down into the first knit stitch at the other side of the panel. When you reach the head of the motif, outline it with a four-sided stitch and move on to the second wing.

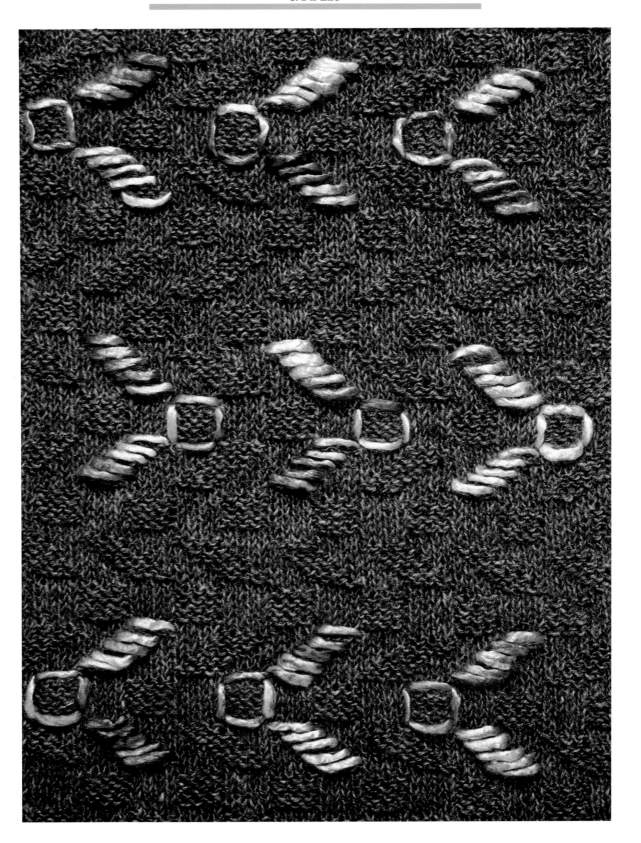

SAMPLE 14

●●●KNITTING●●●
Basket-weave pattern in yarn 24.

●●●EMBROIDERY●●●
Stem stitch in yarn 34.

Some knit-and-purl patterns have such clear structures that there is little difficulty in seeing how to embroider them. This basket weave, with its clever use of the natural curl of knit and purl stitches, is one of them.

The pattern, by introducing a purl stitch in the centre of the vertical knit bands and a knit row in the centre of the horizontal purl bands, offers very clear embroidery lines. The thin knitting yarn, in this case, suggested a thin embroidery line. A long stem stitch seemed a good option.

The embroidery was done in two colours – salmon and sky blue – for several reasons. First, they reflected the many specks in the knitting yarn better than a single colour would have done. Secondly, it was a way of enlarging and adding boldness to the pattern. Finally, a basket weave within a basket weave seemed a rather interesting proposition.

The instructions, on a multiple of 18 stitches plus 7 stitches, read:

row 1 (right side) – k3, p1, *k8, p1, repeat from *, end k3

rows 2 and 4 – p3, k1, p3, *k11, p3, k1, p3, repeat from *

row 3 – k3, p1, k3, *p11, k3, p1, k3, repeat from *

row 5 – k3, p1, *k17, p1, repeat from *, end k3

rows 6 and 8 – like rows 2 and 4

row 7 – like row 3

row 9 – like row 1

rows 10 and 12 – k9, *p3, k1, p3, k11, repeat from *, end last repeat k9

row 11 – p9, *k3, p1, k3, p11, repeat from *, end last repeat p9

row 13 – k12, p1, *k17, p1, repeat from *, end k12

rows 14 and 16 – like rows 10 and 12

row 15 – like row 1

To work the stem stitch, follow the sunken lines in the pattern. For a thin line, catch three or four knitted strands with each stitch. For a thicker, more rope-like line, catch only one or two at a time.

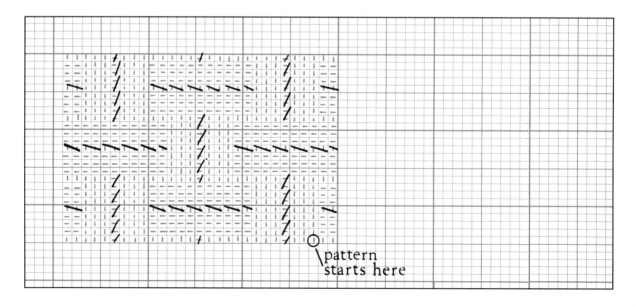

\pattern
starts here

SAMPLE 15

● ● ●KNITTING● ● ●
Triangular pattern in yarn 14.

● ● ●EMBROIDERY● ● ●
Backstitch in yarn 9.

The knitting yarn for this sample is wonderfully rich in colour and texture; there would be no point in knitting complex stitches with it, therefore, because they would not show.

The pattern chosen is quite simple but, by displaying now knit stitches, now purl stitches, it makes a fabric that doesn't curl and blends the colours very successfully. The way in which the stitches lie next to each other, some raised and some sunk, adds movement and makes the fabric very intriguing.

The pattern is nothing more than an arrangement of right-angled triangles, as close to each other as they can be. Pinwheels can be easily identified on a chart, or on samples knitted in smooth yarn. All the embroidery has done is to highlight some of these with backstitch.

The embroidery yarn had to be fairly plain to make a good contrast and show a clear outline. The one chosen, with its uneven twist and rustic looks, blends in very well with the knitting yarn. Its slight changes in thickness and colour echo the rich texture of the other yarn.

The triangles in the chart are six stitches wide. For the sample, these were scaled down to three stitches, owing to the chunkiness of the yarn. Instructions for the larger triangles and for a multiple of 12 stitches read:

rows 1 and 2 – *p6, k6, repeat from *
rows 3 and 4 – *k1, p5, k5, p1, repeat from *
rows 5 and 6 – *k2, p4, k4, p2, repeat from *
rows 7 and 8 – *k3, p3, repeat from *
rows 9 and 10 – *k4, p2, k2, p4, repeat from *
rows 11 and 12 – *k5, p1, k1, p5, repeat from *
rows 13 and 14 – *k6, p6, repeat from *
rows 15 and 16 – *p6, k6, repeat from *
rows 17 and 18 – *p5, k1, p1, k5, repeat from *
rows 19 and 20 – *p4, k2, p2, k4, repeat from *
rows 21 and 22 – *p3, k3, repeat from *
rows 23 and 24 – *p2, k4, p4, k2, repeat from *
rows 25 and 26 – *p1, k5, p5, k1, repeat from *
rows 27 and 28 – *k6, p6, repeat from *

To work the embroidery, choose your pinwheels and outline them with backstitch. Make sure that the centre stitch is shared by the four sides. Knit-stitch pinwheels are easier to see because their long sides are raised. If you want to highlight purl-stitch ones, it might be best to embroider them in a different way – perhaps in satin stitch or another filling stitch.

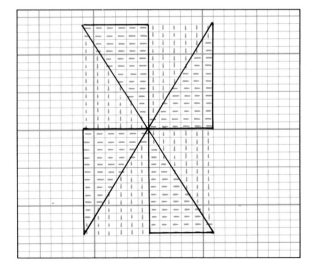

EYELETS

One of the great attractions of eyelets is that they allow thick yarns to go through thin fabrics with great ease. Another is that they can be used to build a grid on fabrics, like those made of stocking stitch, that don't lend themselves easily to embroidered knitting. Once you have a net of eyelets, you can use them as embroidery points. After the work is finished, you might not even see the eyelets any more, but they will have given you the means of embroidering, quickly and accurately, a fabric that would have taken much effort to embroider otherwise.

On certain rows, a sequence of eyelets is introduced. Each eyelet is worked one or more stitches away from the last one. The eyelet rows can be alike or not, depending on what you want to use the grid for. Even if the eyelet sequence is the same, each row might start at a different point in the sequence. In this way, the eyelets can be staggered or they can be made to travel one or two stitches at a time.

The easiest way to make an eyelet is to work two stitches together – knit or purl depending on what side of the work you are on. Just before, or just after you do that, wrap the yarn around the needle to make a 'yarn-over'. On the next row, if you want a large eyelet, purl (or knit) the 'yarn-over' as it comes. If you want a small eyelet, work it twisted.

Making the 'yarn-over' before or after the decrease alters the way in which the fabric turns around the eyelet. If you want to reverse either of these ways, so that the fabric does to the right of the eyelet what it now does to its left, you need to use a decrease slanting in the opposite direction. The conventional way of doing this is:

> slip 1 knitwise, k1, pass slip stitch over.

There is, however, another way of making this kind of decrease which gives much neater results. It is called slip-slip-knit:

> slip 2 stitches knitwise, one at a time; insert the tip of the left needle into them, keeping this needle in front of the right needle; wind the yarn around the right needle, and 'knit' the 2 stitches together.

Try a few samples to decide which eyelets are best for a particular purpose. Until you see them knitted and embroidered, it is often difficult to know which are most suitable.

The embroidery used in the burgundy coat doesn't appear in any of the projects, but the principle behind it is very simple: cable hemstitch is worked onto travelling lines of eyelets. The eyelets are equally spaced on alternate rows, but their position moves one stitch to right or left every time. The background is stocking stitch, and either the knit or the purl side could have been used. The purl side was chosen, despite the fact that the outward curling edges are often a problem with coats and jackets, because on samples the embroidery counteracted the curling tendency, so it seemed worthwhile to take the risk and use purl. But the final edges did curl and a special blocking technique had to be devised. Each edge, well-pinned down, was thoroughly sprayed with water. The knitting was then turned over the edge against its natural tendency, sprayed again, and left to dry.

The coat was hand knitted in chunky merino wool. The centre panels, the cuffs and the collar were worked in a very flat slip-stitch pattern and edged with reverse stocking-stitch rolls. These rolls cover the seams so that the embroidered side pieces can be stitched flat under the centre panels.

The coat was embroidered in a yarn made out of two very lightly twisted strands – one off-white, double but very fine, the other slubby and rainbow dyed.

For full-length view of coat, see page 2.

SAMPLE 16

● ● ● KNITTING ● ● ●

Purl side of stocking stitch with eyelets, in yarn 23.

● ● ● EMBROIDERY ● ● ●

Zigzag chain stitch in the same yarn.

The purl side of stocking stitch was chosen for this sample because it makes the yarn look much more exciting than it does from the knit side: the knobs are more visible and the gleaming ribbon is more prominent. In addition, the colours are as subtly blended as they were in the ball.

The huge embroidery stitches, with their bold long loops, reveal precisely what the yarn looks like before being knitted. Given the complex nature of the yarn, this is a very interesting counterpoint to the purl background.

The eyelet arrangement is very simple. On the eyelet row:

> *k2, k2 together, yarn over, repeat from *.

Repeat every six rows. The eyelets are not staggered.

The embroidery is just as simple. Lines of zigzag chain stitch are worked from top to bottom. They snake between two lines of eyelets in perfect parallel. Zigzag chains moving at cross purposes can be superimposed over all or some of the original chains. In the sample, one has been worked over every third chain.

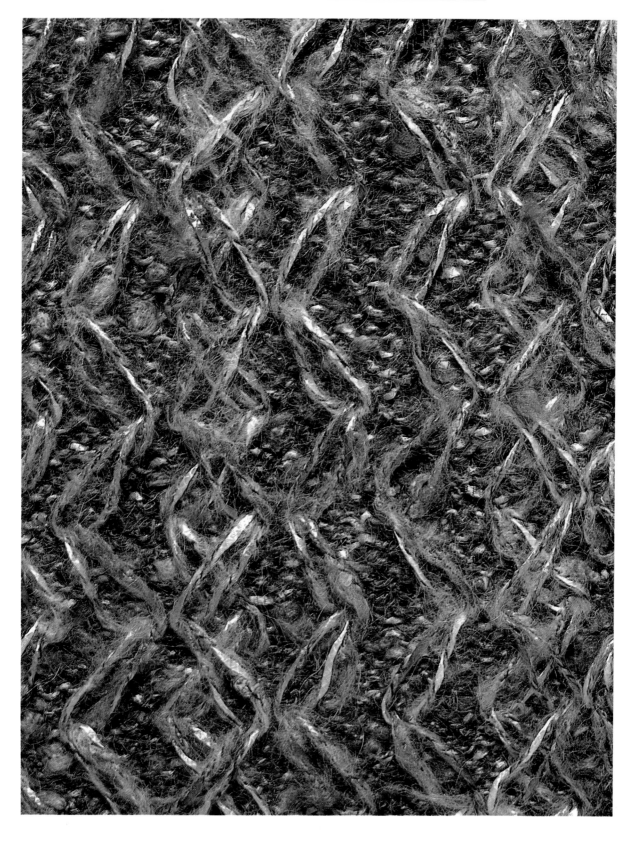

SAMPLE 17

●●●KNITTING●●●

Stocking stitch with eyelets in yarn 3
(machine knitted).

●●●EMBROIDERY●●●

Whipping stitch in yarn 4 (tapestry wool).

Fine, peat-brown Shetland yarn provides a good backcloth for the light-to-dark shades of tapestry wool. Four cool blues and four warm terracottas have been used. In the central area, each one has its own row – cool shades alternating with warm ones. The blues become lighter on their way down; the terracottas become darker. In this way, balance is maintained.

On the top and bottom bands, the colours mingle. At the top, the two lightest blues have been superimposed on the two darkest terracottas. At the bottom, the two lightest terracottas travel over the two darkest blues.

The eyelet sequence is as follows:

*yarn over, k2 together, k4, repeat from *.

Repeat every six rows. The eyelets are not staggered.

The embroidery appears to be zigzag backstitch but, in fact, it is a double line of whipping (as described under whipped running stitch). The way in which the yarn wraps itself around the eyelets with this method was more suitable for the present sample. But this may not always be the case – see blue sweater, p. 35.

To obtain a zigzag with two lines of whipping, work first from right to left, zigzagging along two eyelet rows. Complete the pattern by working from left to right, into the same eyelets.

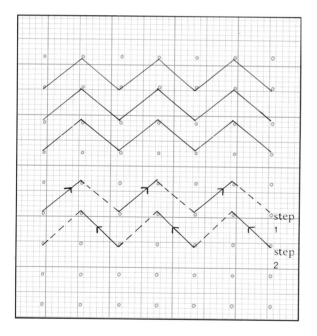

SAMPLE 18

● ● ●KNITTING● ● ●

Stocking stitch with eyelets in yarn 9 (spaced dyed).

● ● ●EMBROIDERY● ● ●

Running stitch in yarns 20 (2 strands), 41 and 45.

This knitting yarn has a fascinating way of changing colour very slowly and subtly, creating dark and light areas in the knitting.

The eyelets are very close together. Only one stitch was knitted between the 'yarn-over' and the decrease from the next eyelet. The eyelet position travels one stitch towards the right on each eyelet row. These two factors, together with the way in which the contrast yarns were to be threaded, pointed towards a slip-slip-knit decrease (as explained on page 23):

*k1, slip-slip-knit, yarn over, repeat from *.

Repeat every four rows, moving the eyelet position one stitch to the right each time.

The embroidery follows the steep diagonals set by the travelling eyelets. In the sample, three contrasting textures of the same shade have been used. Three contrasting shades of the same texture would have been another option. The two yarns with the greatest contrast (in this case the very glossy ribbon and the hazy mohair), were worked side by side. The chenille, half-way between the other two with its special sheen and its deep pile, was used for the broken horizontal lines.

To raise the mohair fibres as much as possible, lengths of yarn were well brushed before they were threaded through. Fibres caught into the eyelets were teased out with the tip of the sewing needle.

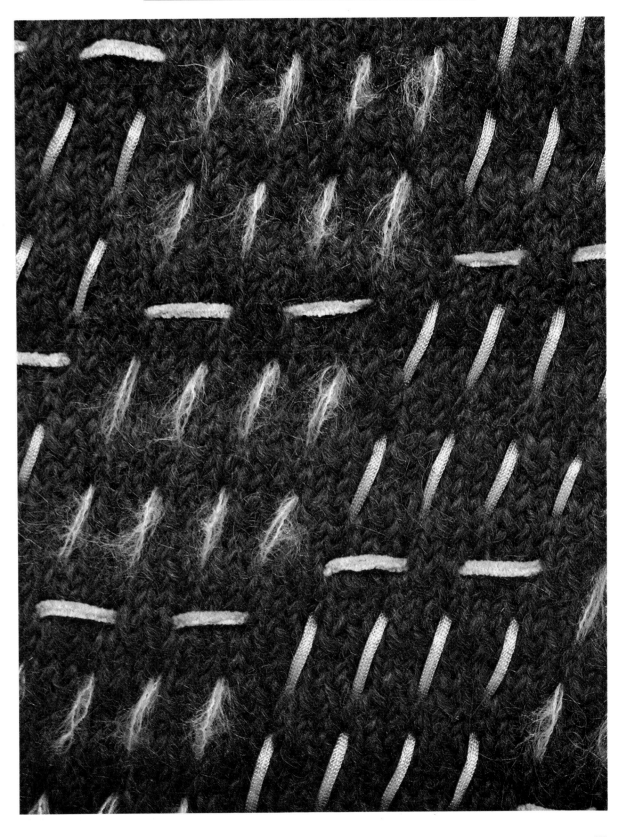

SAMPLE 19

● ● ●KNITTING● ● ●

Stocking stitch with eyelets in yarn 49 (two strands).

● ● ● EMBROIDERY● ● ●

Running stitch in yarn 29.

Each of the two yarns used for this sample has so much character and makes such an impact that even being used in the simplest of ways makes them look stunning.

The knitting yarn is extremely fine and was used double to give it more body. Eyelets were placed just one stitch apart:

> *k1, k2 together, yarn over, repeat from *.

Repeat every four rows. Don't change the eyelet position.

The very thick silk, gleaming even more than usual, owing to the countless reflections from the knitting, is threaded along diagonal lines of eyelets. The bold basket-weave effect works especially well because it causes no strains on the fabric. The heavy silk would have distorted the very soft and light knitting had it been threaded in anything other than straight lines.

SAMPLE 20

● ● ●KNITTING● ● ●
Stocking stitch with eyelets in yarn 37.

● ● ●EMBROIDERY● ● ●
Double cross stitch, with superimposed zigzag backstitch in yarns 37 and 44.

This intricate lattice is far easier to work than it looks. All that it needs is a clever eyelet arrangement.

The eyelets have been worked every six rows. They are all similarly spaced:

> *k2, slip-slip-knit, yarn over, repeat from *.

The slip-slip-knit decrease is explained on page 73. If you are worried about trying it here, work *k2, yarn over, k2 together, instead. The decrease will be at the other side of the eyelet but, in this particular case it will not matter.

What is special about the eyelets in this sample is that their positions are staggered at regular intervals. They are worked in one position for three times. Then they are staggered and they are worked in their new position for a total of three times more. Then they are staggered again, and so on.

When it comes to the embroidery, the double cross stitch is worked first – along the centre lines of two consecutive groups of eyelets. Look at the chart and sample to see the order in which the needle should go in and out of the eyelets, to keep the crosses straight. Leave two empty rows of eyelets in the centre of the crosses – these are the two that are staggered.

With the second embroidery yarn, work zigzag backstitch over the two central eyelet rows. This gives the double-cross stitch a more polished look, and helps to keep down the very long strands made by this stitch.

If two contrasting shades had been used for the embroidery, the stitch structure would show more clearly. But, this time, the idea was not so much to

show how the embroidery progressed, as to create an all-over trellis. The structure is still revealed by the highly contrasting textures of the embroidery yarns, but you have to look closely to realize it.

The more textured yarn, with its sudden knobs and its witty tails, would have been very difficult to embroider without the eyelets. It is a very unusual yarn, fascinating to see in the long lengths afforded by the outsize double-cross stitch. The little tails, rather like tendrils of a climbing plant, go especially well with the trellis effect.

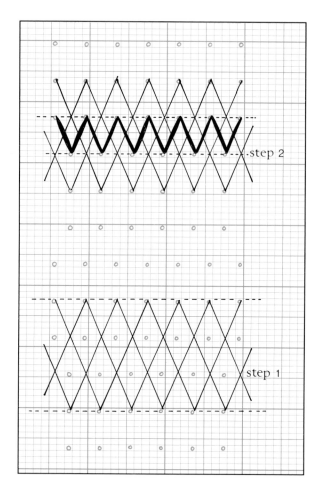

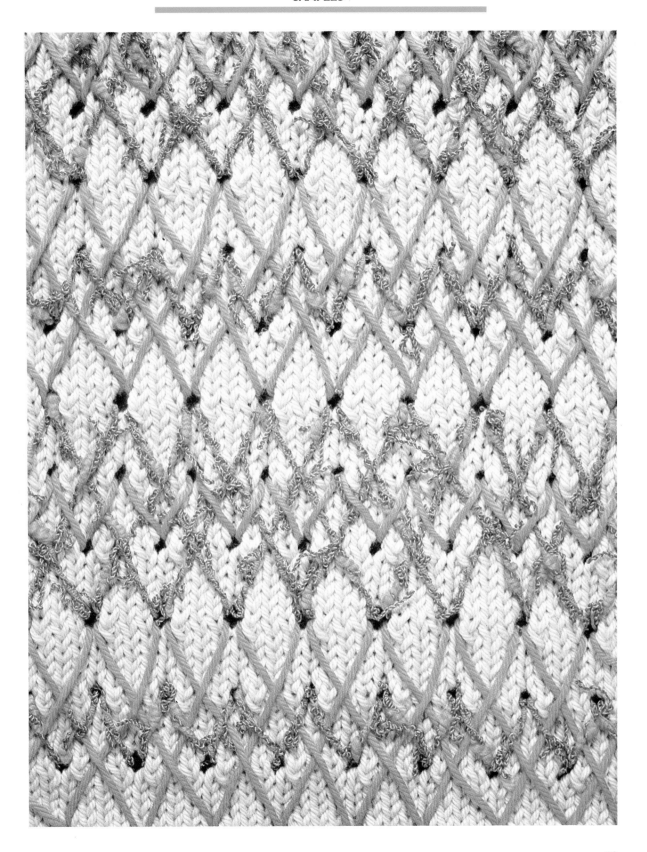

SLIP-STITCH PATTERNS

If you slip a stitch from the left needle to the right needle without working it, and then you knit or purl the next stitch, three things happen. First, the slipped stitch becomes elongated, because it is forced to span an extra row. Secondly, to attain the required length, the slipped stitch pulls yarn from the stitches next to it, on the row below the slip row. Thirdly, a long horizontal strand forms across the elongated stitch, on the slip row.

The long strand shows only on one side of work. If this is the right side, the strand becomes a feature, obscuring the elongated stitch. Otherwise, from the right side you see no sign of the strand and the elongated stitches become the feature.

To have the strand where you want it to be, keep the yarn on the appropriate side of work while slipping the stitch. If, for instance, you are knitting a row and you want the bar to show on the knit side, bring the yarn to front of work before slipping the stitch, and return it to back of work afterwards, so that you can carry on knitting.

Unless the instructions state knitwise, slip all stitches purlwise, to prevent twisting. If you are keeping the strands on the wrong side and want the elongated stitches to rise as much as possible above the background, keep the tension between the stitches you do work almost as tight as if the slip stitch was not there. Most knitters tend to work in this way quite naturally, so you are not likely to have any problems. Remember, however, that every stitch that you slip narrows the width of your knitting. Patterns with slip stitches usually need more stitches than patterns without.

If you want the strand to show on the right side, then you must allow the slip stitch to take up as much room as any other stitch. Therefore, you must be careful not to tighten the strand while slipping it.

Examples of elongated stitches can be seen under **Ribs** – samples 26 and 27. This group deals only in patterns that make use of horizontal strands. Some of these make very clear grids, not unlike moss-stitch grids. Others give geometric arrangements of strands that look woven, and can be embroidered in a variety of ways.

The last kind of pattern can often be dramatically improved with blocking. Lift each strand with a cable or a knitting needle, and give it a gentle jerk to raise it as much as possible above the background. If any stitches pucker, pin them down in their right position. Spray well and then let dry.

SAMPLE 21

● ● ●KNITTING● ● ●
Wasp's nest stitch in yarn 10.

● ● ●EMBROIDERY● ● ●
Whipped running stitch in yarns 10 and 11.

Wasp's nest is a simple stitch giving a very deep fabric, with a surface grid reminiscent of a honeycomb. It does not curl, because it is a slip-stitch development of garter stitch. On alternate rows, every other stitch is slipped. On an odd number of stitches:

rows 1 and 3 (right side) – knit
row 2 – *k1, sl 1 keeping the yarn where it is, repeat from *, k1
row 4 – *sl 1, k1, repeat from *, sl 1

The resulting pattern takes more yarn and grows more slowly than, say, stocking stitch or even garter stitch would, but is wonderfully thick, warm and attractive. It also offers many embroidery possibilities.

The clearest lines are diagonals. Horizontal and vertical lines might be best zigzagged along two rows, or along two lines of stitches. You can burrow diagonally under the long strands, as in sample 25, or use the strands as a base for surface embroidery, as in the present sample.

Lopi wool shows the structure of the pattern very clearly, because of its chunkiness. This yarn is so light that, despite its great thickness, the fabric is not at all heavy.

The sample has been embroidered with whipped running stitch, moving along diagonals – from one long strand to the next. Three shades have been used to create three sets of superimposed squares. Each one of these has nine-strand sides, so that the small squares can have three-strand sides. Complete the squares in one of the colours before moving on to the next colour.

Notice that the whipping has been mirrored along opposing diagonals. Working from the bottom up, whether you are travelling to the right or to the left, always insert the needle into the next strand from the top down.

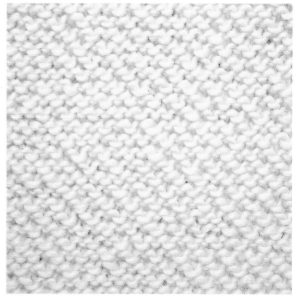

The embroidery doesn't show on the wrong side.

SAMPLE 22

●●●KNITTING●●●
Slip-stitch diagonals in yarn 3 (machine knitted).

●●●EMBROIDERY●●●
Cable hemstitch in yarn 14.

This sample achieves the seemingly impossible: very fine knitting embroidered with a thick, textured and slubby yarn. Not only that – because the embroidery is kept completely on the surface, the structure and the colour of the yarn can be fully appreciated.

All this is possible because three stitches are slipped each time, not just one. All the wrong-side rows are purled, so that no stitches are slipped over more than one row. On the right side, the same sequence of three knit and three slipped stitches is repeated throughout – although it is made to travel one stitch to the left each time. On a multiple of six stitches, the instructions read:

> row 1 and all other wrong-side rows – purl
> row 2 – *sl 3 with yarn in front, k3, repeat from *
> row 4 – k1, *sl 3, k3, repeat from *, end sl 3, k2
> row 6 – k2, *sl 3, k3, repeat from *, end sl 3, k1
> row 8 – *k3, sl 3, repeat from *
> row 10 – sl 1, *k3, sl 3, repeat from *, end k3, sl 2
> row 12 – sl 2, *k3, sl 3, repeat from *, end k3, sl 1

If you prefer, make the pattern travel to the right instead, or create a zigzag.

The embroidery, with its blues and browns, mellows the rather acid yellow of the Shetland yarn. It is worked in cable hemstitch. The long sides of this are wrapped over four Shetland strands. The short central stitches are wrapped over two strands.

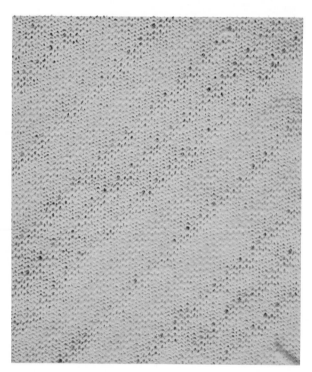

The embroidery doesn't show on the wrong side.

SAMPLE 23

● ● ●KNITTING ● ● ●
Slip-stich zigzags in yarn 6.

● ● ●EMBROIDERY ● ● ●
Threaded backstitch in yarn 15.

Aran wool always gives very clear stitches. In this case, the slip-stitch strands show especially clearly because they are raised by the embroidery. The vibrant shades of the embroidery yarn, and the close way in which the slubs follow the knitting sequence, make this a very dramatic sample.

The knitting is a variation of the diagonals in sample 22. Two stitches are slipped each time instead of three. These travel in opposite directions until they are only one stitch away from each other, at which point they change direction. On a multiple of 16 stitches plus one stitch:

row 1 and all other wrong-side rows – purl
row 2 – k1, *slip 2 (all stitches are slipped with yarn in front), k11, sl 2, k1, repeat from *
row 4 – k2, *sl 2, k9, sl 2, k3, repeat from *, end last repeat k2
row 6 – k3, *sl 2, k7, sl 2, k5, repeat from *, end last repeat k3
row 8 – k4, *sl 2, k5, sl 2, k7, repeat from *, end last repeat k4
row 10 – k5, *sl 2, k3, sl 2, k9, repeat from *, end last repeat k5
row 12 – k6, *sl 2, k1, sl 2, k11, repeat from *, end last repeat k6
row 14 – like row 10
row 16 – like row 8
row 18 – like row 6
row 20 – like row 4

Notice that the lines of slip stitches zigzag but never cross. Only the embroidery crosses from one line to the next, transforming the zigzags into a kind of hexagonal mesh.

Embroider in threaded backstitch, down a right-to-left diagonal. At the first corner, jump to the next diagonal with a horizontal stitch. Continue in this way along all the right-to-left lines, then work from left to right, mirroring the twist of the stitches.

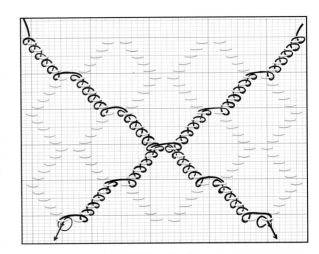

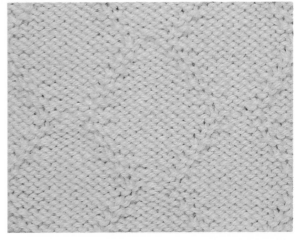

The embroidery doesn't show on the wrong side.

SAMPLE 24

● ● ●KNITTING● ● ●

Slip-stitch zigzags in yarn 4 (double knitting).

● ● ●EMBROIDERY● ● ●

Backstitch in yarn 4 (tapestry wool).

In this sample, two stitches are slipped on every row giving a very compact line of slip-stitch strands. Each of these two stitches is slipped on two consecutive rows. Therefore, it needs to span three rows rather than two, and tends to pull its neighbours more than usual.

Keep the strands quite long, block the knitting carefully, and all will be well.

Instructions for the sample, on a multiple of nine stitches plus one stitch, read:

row 1 (right side) – *slip 2 (all right-side stitches are slipped with yarn in front of work), k7, repeat from *, sl 1

row 2 – *p7, sl 2 (all wrong-side stitches are slipped with yarn at back of work), repeat from *, p1

row 3 – k2, *sl 2, k7, repeat from *, end last repeat k6

row 4 – p5, *sl 2, k7, repeat from *, end last repeat p3

row 5 – k4, *sl 2, k7, repeat from *, end last repeat k4

row 6 – p3, *sl 2, p7, repeat from *, end last repeat p5

row 7 – k6, *sl 2, k7, repeat from *, end last repeat k2

row 8 – p1, *sl 2, p7, repeat from *, end last repeat p7

row 9 – sl 1 *k7, sl 2, repeat from *

rows 10 to 16 – repeat rows 8 to 2 in reverse order

The embroidery balances the vertical character of the zigzags by highlighting opposing corners in contrasting shades. The light-to-dark effects possible with tapestry wool are hinted at if you use slightly darker shades in alternate vertical arrangements.

Work one backstitch over each knitted stitch. In the sample, the three stitches either side of each corner were embroidered.

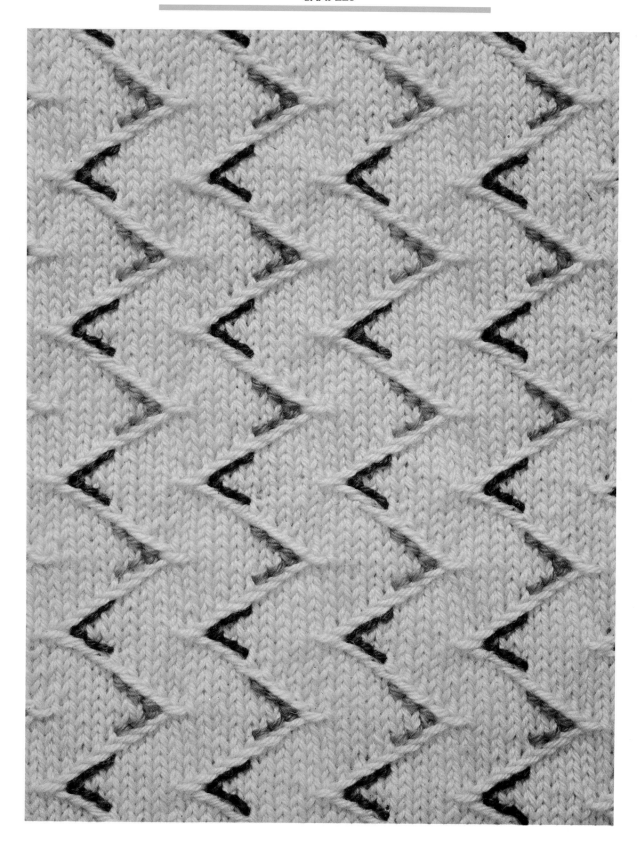

SAMPLE 25

● ● ●KNITTING● ● ●

Wasp's nest stitch in yarn 13.

● ● ●EMBROIDERY● ● ●

Running stitch in yarn 9 (two strands).

Wasp's nest stitch has been described under sample 21. The present sample gives a much smaller version of it, with a certain crinkliness caused by the spiral structure of the knitting yarn.

The soft embroidery yarn was used double to fill the 'cells' of the honeycomb. The double line created in this way, with its twin highlights and its central shadow, add an extra element of interest.

Rich blues and greens were chosen for the slanted chequerboard, and arranged in bands.

Work from the chart. Along each knitted row, eight embroidered cells alternate with seven empty cells.

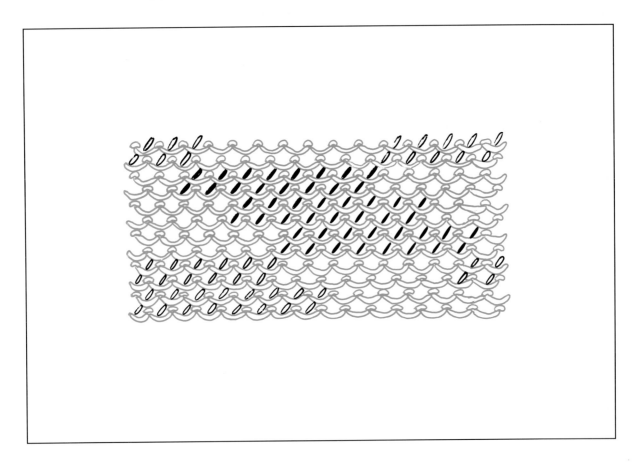

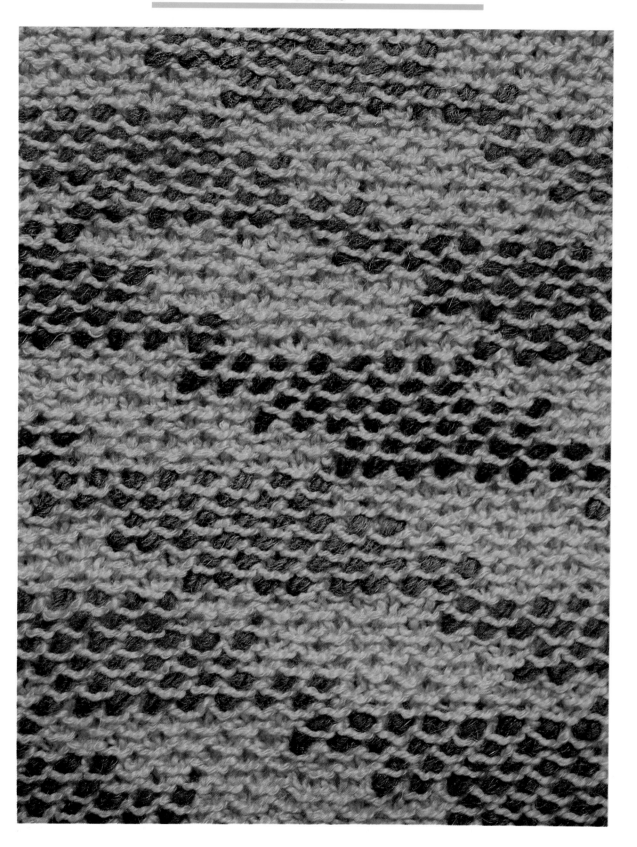

RIBS

Ribs, or ribbings, are patterns with thin vertical lines, like the k1, p1, or k2, p2 ribs that edge so many sweaters. Many other ones exist – not all of them with the same hugging qualities as the two just mentioned.

The present group of samples includes the less elastic ribs. Ideas for embroidering the others can be found under **Borders** – samples 37 to 40.

In this section, first come two examples of ribs worked with the slip-stitch technique explained on page 85. Then there are three examples of smocking.

Smocking is one of the rare types of embroidered knitting that can sometimes be found in books. The general inclination, however, is simply to show equally-spaced rows of honeycomb stitch. Accepting all the limitations of a knitted fabric, it is high time that a few more lessons were learnt from the great British smocking tradition.

SAMPLE 26

● ● ●KNITTING● ● ●
Slip-stitch rib in yarn 31.

● ● ●EMBROIDERY● ● ●
Threaded running stitch in yarn 41, cross stitch in yarn 22 (four strands), and four-sided stitch in yarn 43.

The very interesting knitting yarn used for this sample required a simple stitch – possibly with a purl background, to make the most of all the curls and knobs. A k1, p5 rib was adopted, but the knitted stitches were slipped on alternate rows to raise them above the background, and make them easier to count. On a multiple of six stitches plus five stitches:

row 1 (wrong side) – k5, *p1, k5, repeat from *
row 2 – p5, *slip 1 with yarn at back, p5, repeat from *

A striking aspect of this rather complex yarn is the different colour and texture of its two strands. The sage-green wool is soft and lustrous. The golden silk glistens next to it, and the mossy texture casts so many shadows that the two original shades turn into a dozen.

The embroidery had to reflect this colour game, and it does so by using three different yarns in shades that could not blend better with the knitting. First of all, a threaded running stitch is worked in thick, dark chenille along the slip stitches. The order of threading alternates – one rib is started from right to left, and the next one from left to right. This raises the slip stitches further, while paving the way for the embroidery of the cross stitches.

Because of the alternate threading, you can take any pair of opposite chenille loops for the lower points of the first cross. Three loops further up are the top points. The bottom of the next cross to the left is half a loop down from the top of the first cross, and so on. Along a vertical line, there are four free loops between crosses.

The oversized crosses were worked twice over the same points with four strands of angora. The final eight strands give the crosses highlights and shadows that would not have been obtained with a single thick yarn. To keep the long arms in position, a four-sided stitch was worked on the centre with a fine viscose and cotton yarn – itself a blend of matt and glossy threads, like the knitting yarn.

SAMPLE 27

● ● ●KNITTING● ● ●
Double slip-stitch rib, in yarn 15.

● ● ● EMBROIDERY● ● ●
Threaded backstitch in yarn 21 (two strands).

Don't let this very deceptive stitch mislead you; it is not k2, p2 rib. The knit stitches lie too flat for that and, besides, some are much larger than others – although, in this case, it is hard to tell how much that is due to the slub yarn.

A purl stitch can be found hiding between the knit stitches. These, in turn, are slipped alternately on two consecutive rows. On a multiple of six stitches plus three stitches, the instructions read:

> row 1 (right side) – *p3, sl 1 with yarn at back, p1, k1, repeat from *, p3
> row 2 – *k3, p1, k1, sl 1 with yarn in front, repeat from *, k3
> row 3 – *p3, k1, p1, sl 1 with yarn at back, repeat from *, p3
> row 4 – *k3, sl 1 with yarn in front, k1, p1, repeat from *, k3

With a plain yarn, a distinct and very attractive arrangement of small and large stitches appears. In this case, the thick-and-thin yarn can make an ordinary knit stitch look bigger than a slipped one, and vice versa. However, despite the distortion, the pattern was right for the yarn because the aim was to display the many vibrant colours unusually.

Two strands of brushed lustre wool were used for the embroidery. The delicate colour variations of this yarn reflect the many greens in the knitting yarn.

One row of threaded backstitch was worked at either side of alternate ribs, wound around the small stitches. To the right of the rib, work progresses in the usual way. To the left of the rib, it travels in the opposite direction – from right to left – to give symmetrical loops. The lustre wool was well brushed after the work was finished.

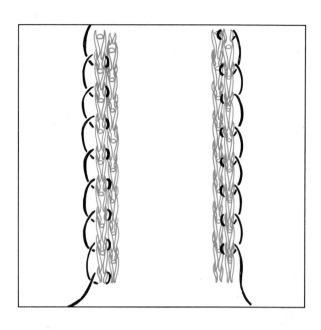

Neither the embroidery nor the ribs show on the wrong side, which looks rather like stocking stitch.

SAMPLE 28

● ● ●KNITTING● ● ●

Knit-stitch rib in yarn 2 (machine knitted).

● ● ●EMBROIDERY● ● ●

Honeycomb stitch and chevron stitch in yarn 3
(two strands).

This sample provides a very nice example of how
superbly the shades of Shetland yarn blend with each
other. The knitting yarn might seem a plain green, but
it is a blend of many shades – separately dyed and
then spun together. The primrose yellow and the
sorbet orange in the embroidery, by picking up
tenuous colour suggestions in the green yarn, are a
good complement to it.

The knitting is simply a k1, p4 rib. Because
smocking gathers the fabric, the sample was worked
much wider than necessary. The only way to assess
how much width will be lost is by embroidering a
sample. In this case about a quarter of the width
was lost.

A double strand of yarn was used for the embroidery, and each honeycomb dot was worked three
times, rather than two, to make it bolder.

All embroidery rows span six knitted rows. Starting
at the centre, this sequence was followed:

> 2 rows of honeycomb stitch in orange
> 2 knitted rows below, 1 row in yellow
> 4 knitted rows below, 1 row in orange
> 6 knitted rows below, 1 row of chevron stitch
> in yellow; the bars at top and bottom of the
> chevron stitch were worked twice, not once
> 2 rows below, 1 row of chevron stitch in
> orange

The last four rows were repeated, in inverted order,
at the top.

The only difference between ordinary chevron
stitch and the smocking version is the way in which the
horizontal bars are made to gather the fabric. On the
second row, the needle was inserted into the top
stitches under the long strands of the first row.

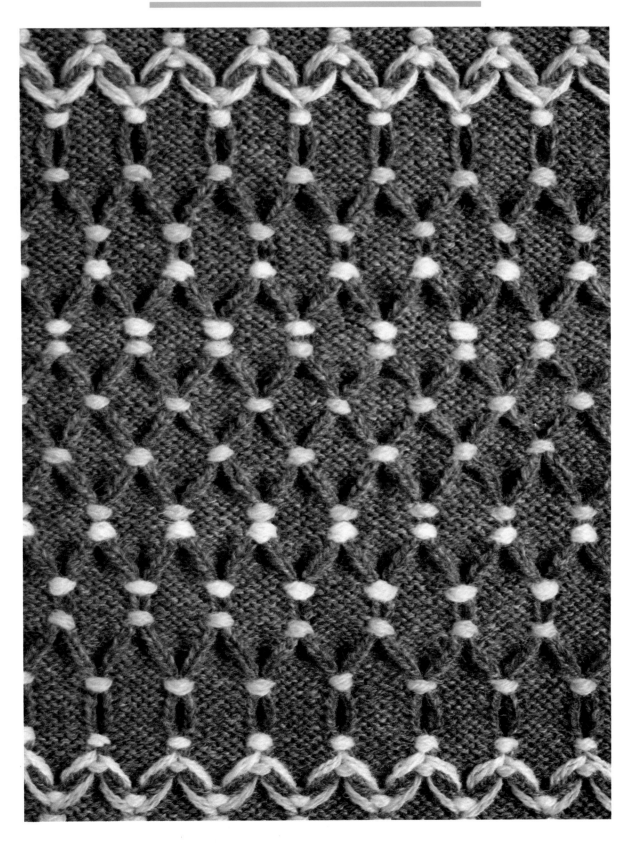

SAMPLE 29

●●●KNITTING●●●
Knit-stitch rib in yarn 47.

●●●EMBROIDERY●●●
Vandyke stitch in yarn 29.

Superimposing and staggering a few rows of vandyke stitch produced this stunning sample. A strong and thick embroidery yarn was essential for it, and this silk could not have been a better choice – especially with the sparkling knitting yarn that lies beneath it.

The knitting is the same k1, p4 rib used in sample 28, but the embroidery rows span 10 knitted rows. As in the other sample, much width was lost while smocking.

Work first a pale row, moving points 1 and 3 to the next knit line to the left. Work a dark row on the points not used by the pale row, so that the two rows cross each other. Work a second set of pale and dark rows, to mirror the first pair, two knitted rows above or below. Then, repeat all four rows 10 knitted rows above or below.

The embroidery doesn't show on the wrong side.

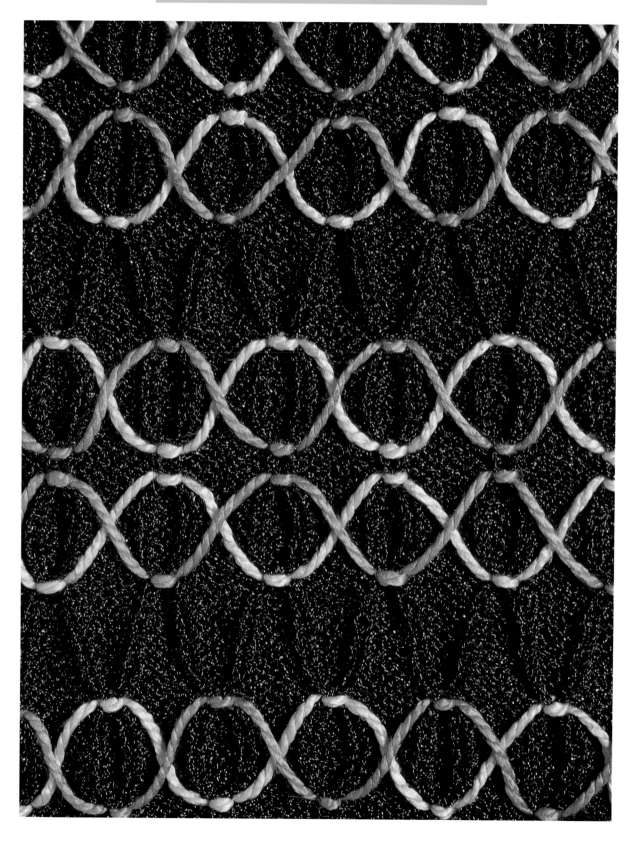

SAMPLE 30

● ● ●KNITTING● ● ●
Corded rib in yarn 9.

● ● ●EMBROIDERY● ● ●
Stem stitch in yarn 34.

This is an unusual rib, that lends itself very well to this very simple kind of smocking.

A soft, thick and light yarn was chosen as a backcloth for 18 of the most delicate shades of stranded embroidery cotton. These were gathered in colour groups that become lighter as they move up.

The rib is based on an increase and decrease sequence. On a multiple of three stitches plus two stitches:

> row 1 (right side) – *p2, k1, repeat from *, p2
> row 2 – *k2, sl 1 with yarn in front, take yarn back over the needle, repeat from *, k2
> row 3 – *p2, k the slip stitch and the yarn over from row 2 together, through the back of the loops, repeat from *, p2
> repeat rows 2 and 3 only.

The embroidery doesn't show on the wrong side.

Block the fabric so that it is well stretched before embroidering. Work along rows in stem stitch, catching the large, slanted rib stitches of alternate rows, and pulling them together to gather the fabric.

Don't be alarmed if the knitting curls. Dampen the wrong side well, pin it right side up, dampen the right side, let it dry, and it will curl no longer.

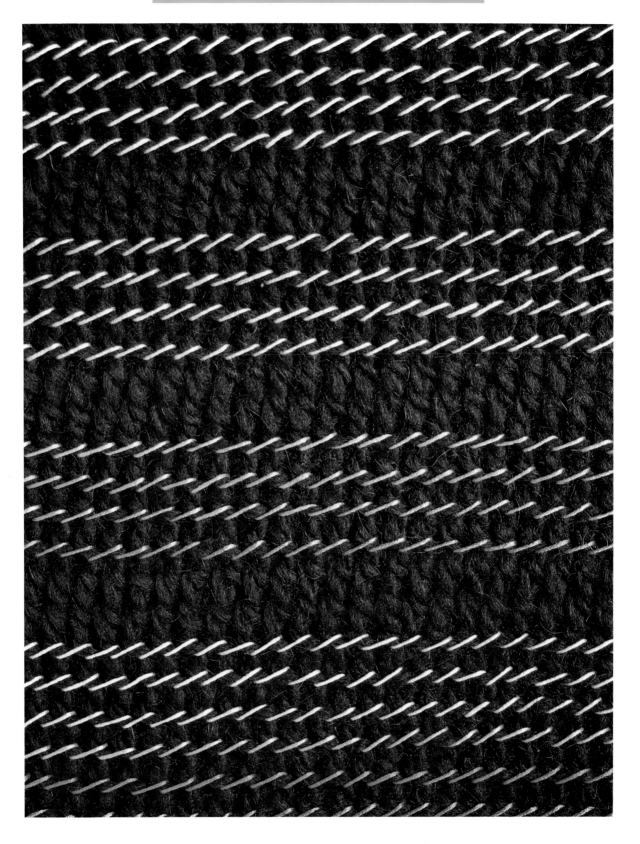

CABLES

With their twisting and turning ropes, cables make very attractive knitting patterns and offer much scope for embroidery. Either the ropes or the background can be added to, depending on the pattern, the yarns, and your intentions.

Cables are fun to work. Some travel across the background until they find another one coming the opposite way. Others move straight up in pairs or groups, twisting around each other from time to time. Either way, most cables are crossed by slipping a few stitches onto a short, double-pointed needle – called a 'cable' needle. The following stitches are then worked as close as possible to the ones already on the right needle. Meanwhile, the cable needle is kept either at front of work, for a right-to-left cross, or at back of work, for a left-to-right cross. Finally, the cable-needle stitches are worked. If you find it awkward to work these stitches directly from the cable needle, slip them back to the left needle.

SAMPLE 31

● ● ● KNITTING ● ● ●
Small mock cable in yarn 24.

● ● ● EMBROIDERY ● ● ●
Running stitch in yarn 28.

This neat little cable is worked without a cable needle. It is based on a k3, p3 rib. On every sixth row, the knit stitches are crossed by working them in reverse order – first the third stitch, then the second, and finally the first.

The tweedy knitting yarn has quite a few specks and fibre blobs – pale green, purple, dark brick, navy – and quite a sheen, owing to its high silk content. Both these factors are reflected in the thick, highly-coloured embroidery silk, as it weaves its way in and out of the cable crossings.

Work in running stitch, over two rows of cable crossings, alternating one from the top row and one from the lower row. This is all.

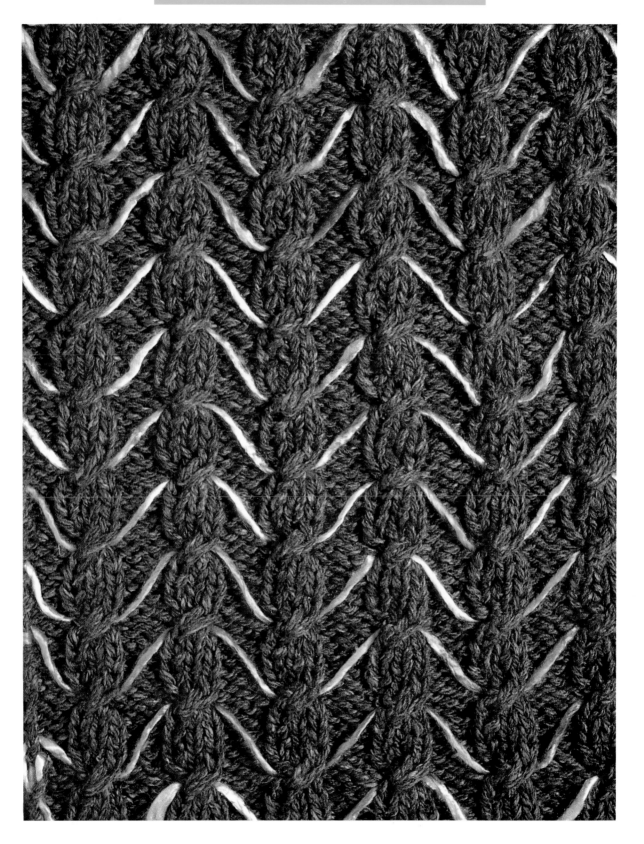

SAMPLE 32

● ● ●KNITTING● ● ●
Straight lattice in yarn 2 (machine knitted).

● ● ●EMBROIDERY● ● ●
Stem stitch in yarn 3 (4 strands).

This knitting yarn is a very variegated example of Shetland wool mixture. Two of the many shades have been picked up for the embroidery. The primrose yellow follows the top line of the cables as a highlight. The peat brown follows the bottom line as a shadow.

At the centre of the diamonds, the three knit stitches of the cables need to be kept an even number of stitches apart – 14 in the sample. Every other cable travels one stitch to the right on every right-side row. The rest of the cables travel one stitch to the left. When two cables meet, they cross each other and continue travelling in their original directions. All cables cross from left to right on the first crossing row, and from right to left on the next crossing row. This creates the woven trellis effect of the sample. On wrong-side rows, knit the knit stitches and purl the purl stitches as they come.

Each cable has been outlined with two rows of stem stitch. Four strands of yarn were taken together to make thick, bold ropes nearly as wide as the knitted cables.

SAMPLE 33

● ● ●KNITTING● ● ●

Stocking-stitch cable in yarn 25.

● ● ●EMBROIDERY● ● ●

Zigzag backstitch in yarn 48.

Most cable patterns make their ropes stand out on a purl background; this one doesn't. In essence, it is nothing more than stocking stitch with crossings on every fourth row. On a multiple of 12 stitches plus two stitches:

> row 1 and all other wrong-side rows – purl
> row 2 – knit
> row 4 – k1, *cross 4 left-to-right (place 2 sts on cable needle, keep at back of work, k2, then k the 2 from the cable needle), k4, cross 4 right-to-left (as before, but keep the cable needle at front of work), repeat from *, k1
> row 6 – knit
> row 8 – k1, *k2, cross 4 right-to-left, cross 4 left-to-right, k2, repeat from *, k1.

The resulting fabric has some very clear-cut shadows right under the cable crossings, asking to be emphasized with a few dark embroidery stitches. This is done with an inverted 'V' in zigzag backstitch, topped with a horizontal stitch, as shown in the diagram. This last stitch is needed because the crossing tends to produce a small hole in the fabric, and this makes the top of the inverted 'V' look rather untidy.

Four strands of very fine silk were used together to make a chunkier yarn and to blend the many shades of green in a smooth and subtle way.

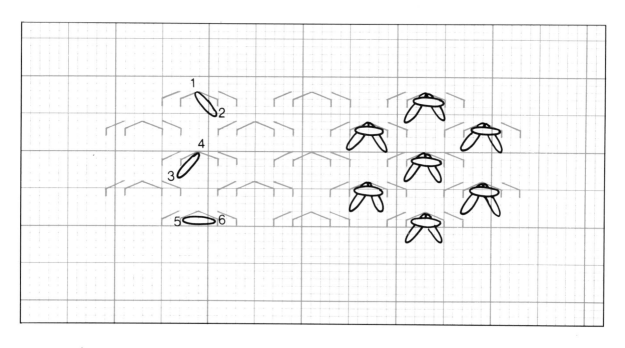

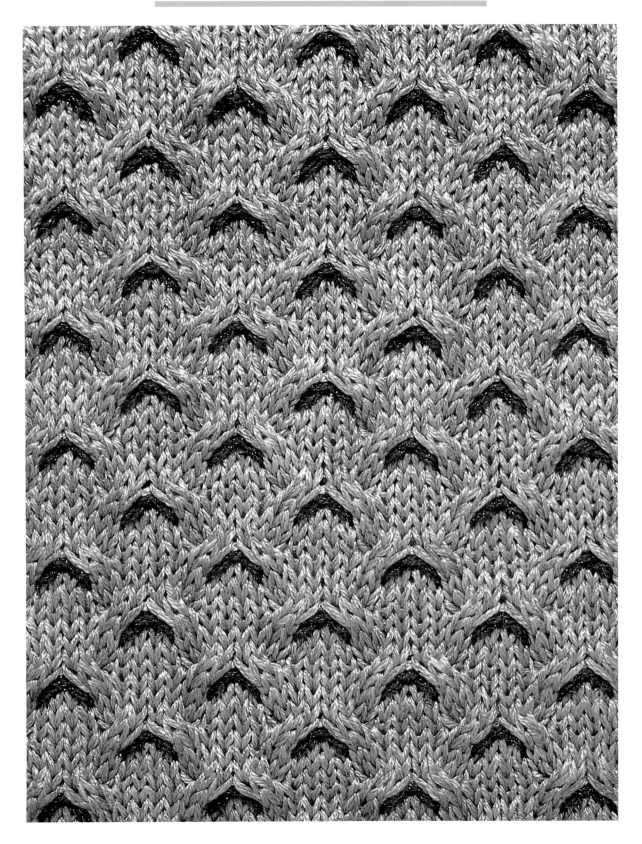

SAMPLE 34

●●●KNITTING●●●
Double cable in yarn 37.

●●●EMBROIDERY●●●
Running stitch and whipped running stitch in yarn 43 (two strands).

This cotton double-knitting yarn gives well-raised, rounded cable ropes. There are really two cables, intertwined in a fascinating manner. The double strand of shiny running stitch, riding high on top of the cables, makes them stand out even more from the background. And, by using two distinct shades, it clarifies the cable paths. See the chart for exact details of how the cables travel.

The little insertions at the sides are nothing more than one garter stitch, flanked by one knit stitch on each side. Knit the three stitches on right-side rows; p1, k1, p1 on wrong-side rows. To embroider, catch the bumps of the garter stitches with a whipped running stitch. Work this in the usual way on the insertion to the right of the cables, and in the opposite direction on the insertion to the left.

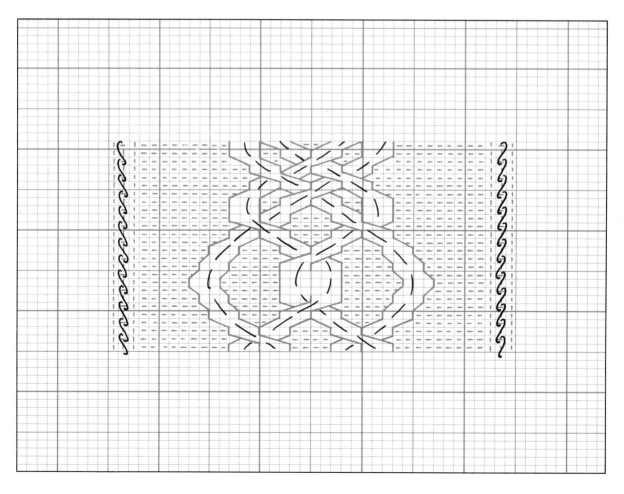

SAMPLE 35

● ● ● KNITTING ● ● ●

Double ribbon stitch in yarn 2.

● ● ● EMBROIDERY ● ● ●

Running stitch in yarn 11, and satin stitch in yarns 9 (two strands) and 10.

This little hourglass cable has such clear, round holes that it was tempting to turn the holes into fun, coloured buttons. This was done by filling the holes in satin stitch in two very light but chunky wools. Because one wool is thicker than the other, the number of the stitches needed to fill a circle varies. The finer wool was used double to speed up the embroidery.

Eight shades were used to embroider the holes, picking up some of the specks in the Shetland mixture, and adding a few new ones.

To lift the hourglass further from the background, a running stitch in grey, tweedy lopi wool was worked on the sides.

To work the cable, on a multiple of 12 stitches plus four stitches (which leaves four purl stitches between cables):

row 1 and all other wrong-side rows – *k4, p8, repeat from *, k4
row 2 – *p4, cross 4 left-to-right (as in sample 33), cross 4 right-to-left, repeat from *, p4
row 4 – *p4, k8, repeat from *, p4
row 6 – *p4, cross 4 right-to-left, cross 4 left-to-right, repeat from *, p4
row 8 – *p4, k8, repeat from *, p4

SAMPLE 36

●●●KNITTING●●●
Cable lattice in yarn 41.

●●●EMBROIDERY●●●
Running stitch in yarn 32.

Cables worked in chenille are not quite as distinctive as they would be knitted in a plainer yarn. This characteristic, added to the delicate greyish green, and the neat hexagons made by the pattern, made a darker background desirable.

A yarn with an unusual twist was chosen for the embroidery. Its ropiness seemed an appropriate way of reflecting the knitted cables.

The running stitch picks up the top loop of every fourth purl stitch. These are caught alternately, on successive embroidery rows, to create a basket-weave impression.

To knit this pattern, start with a p6, k4 sequence. Cross the knit stitches three times, every six rows. Divide the two arms of the cable, and make them travel in opposite directions, one stitch on every right-side row, until they meet another rope coming from the other side. See the chart for exact details.

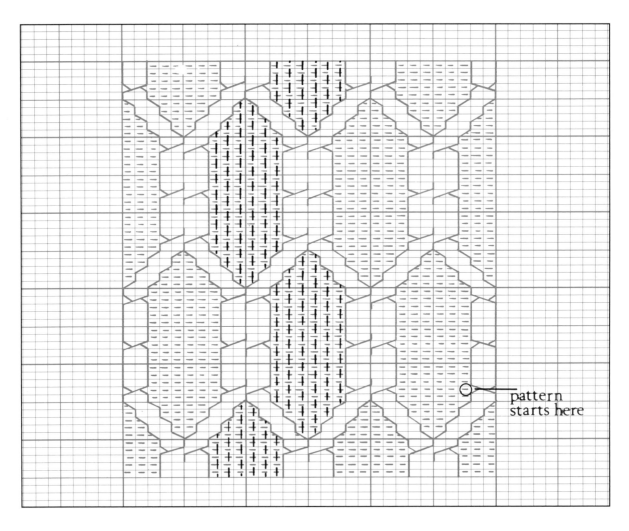

pattern
starts here

BORDERS

The edges of a piece of knitting are very often different from the rest. By adding embroidery to these edges, you can make them even more different.

If the rest of the knitting is also embroidered, the borders can reflect the general embroidery theme. If it is not, then they can be turned into the main design feature.

The examples that follow suggest ways in which borders can be used to edge plain fabrics, knitted in different kinds of yarn. Four of these borders are in the ever popular k1, p1 and k2, p2 ribs.

SAMPLE 37

●●●KNITTING●●●
k1, p1 rib and stocking stitch in yarn 8.

●●●EMBROIDERY●●●
Backstitch in yarn 7 (two strands).

A very straightforward k1, p1 rib, followed by stocking stitch in thick, tweedy wool. The variegated yarn is very attractive and thick enough for the stitches to show clearly.

The embroidery was done in a finer version of the same yarn. Two strands of this were used in preference to a single, thick strand, to obtain a double line of stitches that look rather like coffee beans.

The blue embroidery yarn matches some of the specks in the knitting yarn, and has specks of its own, which, in turn, are reflected by the other two embroidery yarns. Together, the three yarns brighten up the knitting considerably.

Work in backstitch over every line of knit stitches in the ribbing, spanning two rows each time. Use three shades in rotation, and prolong every fourth line into the stocking stitch area. These longer lines repeat the colour sequence established over the ribbing.

Allow for the ribbing to widen and lose some of its elasticity.

SAMPLE 38

●●●KNITTING●●●

k1, p1 rib and reverse stocking stitch in yarn 16.

●●●EMBROIDERY●●●

Chain stitch and threaded running stitch in yarn 30.

The regular slubs of the extra-chunky knitting yarn tend to set into patterns. In this ribbing, they naturally produced alternating lines of very large and very small knit stitches, separated by much more evenly-sized purl stitches. The effect is reversed on the other side, which looks not unlike sample 27. The purl side of stocking stitch was used because it makes the shades blend better and the slubs look more prominent.

The embroidery yarn was selected for its colour – being a deeper shade than the flesh tones in the knitting yarn but in perfect harmony with them. Its sheen and texture, in crisp contrast with the smooth slub, were an added benefit.

The small knit lines were simply embroidered in threaded running stitch. The large ones had a chain stitch worked along their centre first, and then the running stitch was threaded in and out of the chains.

SAMPLE 39

●●●KNITTING●●●

k2, p2 rib and stocking stitch in yarn 18 (two strands).

●●●EMBROIDERY●●●

Zigzag backstitch in yarn 33.

The rather fine mohair was knitted double to increase its bulk. The main attraction of this perfectly straight-forward piece of knitting was the rich, jewel colour. The six vibrant shades of the embroidery are a bold and uncompromising addition. They give a new dimension to the knitting yarn, not only through their colours, but also through their texture. A slightly rough pure linen would not automatically be associated with vaporous mohair, and yet they make a stunning complement to each other.

For the embroidery, work in zigzag backstitch along the double knit lines. Consecutive points are two rows apart on neighbouring knit lines and right in the centre of the stitch.

Prolong the embroidery into the stocking stitch for 8, 6 and 4 extra oblique lines. End each row with a vertical stitch, to turn the last two lines into a triangle.

SAMPLE 40

●●●KNITTING●●●

k2, p2 rib and stocking stitch in yarn 4
(double knitting).

●●●EMBROIDERY●●●

Whipping stitch in yarn 4 (tapestry wool).

This is another plain piece of knitting transformed by embroidery, this time in four dark-to-light shades of tapestry wool.

You can either plan this kind of pattern beforehand and knit an appropriate number of rows, or adapt the pattern to the number of rows that you find yourself having. In the second case, you could have some blocks larger than the others.

Start the embroidery at the bottom of each knit rib, on the right-hand stitch. Work up, always on the right side of the rib. At the top, take the yarn to the left side and work down.

The embroidery is rather like whipped running stitch, but it is worked vertically; insert the needle sideways into the knit stitches, one at a time. This must always be done from right to left, which automatically mirrors the stitch as you work one side up and the other side down. The shades are arranged in waves – gradually from light to dark, and to light again.

To whip the edge, work first with the lightest shade, catching every other stitch. Then, work in the opposite direction with the darkest shade, catching the stitches left on the first row.

SAMPLE 41

● ● ● KNITTING ● ● ●

Welting and reverse stocking stitch, in yarn 17.

● ● ● EMBROIDERY ● ● ●

Chain stitch in yarn 3 (two strands).

This amusing yarn is attractive when viewed from both sides of work, but the confetti-like blobs stand out more from the background on the purl side. This side was therefore chosen.

To carry on the purl theme, welting (as explained for sample 6) was used as a border. This time, however, the knit deep band is narrower than the purl high band. The sequence followed reads:

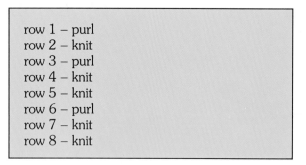

```
row 1 – purl
row 2 – knit
row 3 – purl
row 4 – knit
row 5 – knit
row 6 – purl
row 7 – knit
row 8 – knit
```

On row 8 of the last repeat, an increase was worked on every fourth stitch, to gather the main fabric.

A row of chain stitch was worked along each groove. Two strands of forest-green Shetland wool were used. Each chain was two-and-a-half to three knitted stitches long – it was difficult to tell exactly because of the variations in the knitting.

The chains head, alternately, to right and left. In the very dark green colour used it doesn't matter much which way they go, but in lighter colours the change in direction would have added movement to the embroidery.

SAMPLE 42

● ● ●KNITTING● ● ●

Garter stitch and stocking stitch in yarn 41.

● ● ●EMBROIDERY● ● ●

Running stitch in yarns 2 and 3 (four strands).

Garter stitch and chenille go especially well together, as they give a fabric not unlike corduroy. Chenille also produces an interesting effect with stocking stitch, which it makes look as no other yarn does. From a distance, it is rather like unstretched k1, p1 rib, but what looks like the dividing lines made by the purl stitches in ribbing are the centre lines of the knit stitches.

In the sample, the garter stitch has been embroidered with bundles of four strands of Shetland wool: three light-to-dark shades of tangerine, and two mixtures in pale shades of the knitted bottle green.

Moving down from the centre of the small triangles at the top of the border, the colours run as follows:

dark tangerine
light tangerine
no embroidery
pale green
no embroidery
light tangerine
medium tangerine
dark tangerine
pale green
light tangerine
medium tangerine
dark tangerine
dark green
light tangerine
medium tangerine
dark tangerine
no embroidery
dark green
no embroidery
dark tangerine
light tangerine

The zigzags change direction after burrowing under seven garter-stitch ridges. The pattern covers a total of 17 ridges, or 34 rows, above the cast on.

On the wrong side, only yarn tails show around the edges. A similar pattern worked all over would not show on the wrong side.

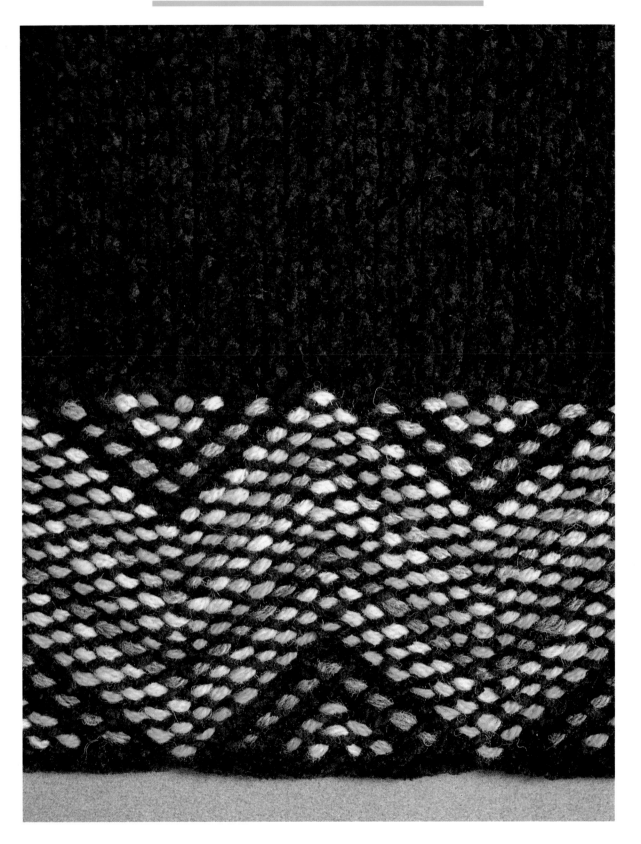

SEAMS

Like borders, seams can be embroidered so that they echo the embroidery done in other areas, or so that they become a feature in their own right. Most of the seams in this group have been knitted with embroidery in mind. Some of them could also be worked without help from the knitting, but it would be harder.

The samples show three vertical seams, two diagonal or raglan seams, and one horizontal seam. Many of these are interchangeable. Others could be adapted to a new situation by seeing in what way the knitting helps the embroidery, and finding a substitute way. The decreases of sample 47, for example, could become purl stitches in a vertical or horizontal situation. The embroidery of samples 43, 44 or 45

could be worked on a raglan seam if this had a decrease band like the one in sample 46.

To make sure that seams are straight, perfectly tidy and easy to sew, follow the techniques outlined on page 24.

Embroidering a seam might stiffen it. If necessary, pin it down, dampen it very well and let it dry. This will remove most of the stiffness. The rest is due to the added layers of yarn and has to be accepted. In many cases it will not matter, especially if you have designed the knitting bearing this in mind. If, however, you want certain seams to remain light and supple, don't embroider them, or use very light yarn and one of the running stitches.

SAMPLE 43

● ● ●KNITTING ● ● ●
Stocking stitch with vertical ladder-stitch seam in yarn 24 (machine knitted).

● ● ●EMBROIDERY ● ● ●
Stem stitch in yarn 35.

This is an ordinary seam, requiring no preparation at knitting stage. It is essential to sew it with a ladder stitch because the join must be one hundred per cent straight.

Following the centre line of the stitch next to the seam line, work a row of stem stitch – one embroidery

stitch over each knitted stitch. Repeat one stitch away from the seam line, pulling the needle from the other side of the yarn to reverse the effect. Repeat on the other side of the seam, mirroring the first two rows.

Two maize shades were alternated in the sample. They are paler versions of some of the specks in the knitting yarn, purposely pale to increase the contrast with the nearly-black navy. A cabled cotton was used because its special twist gives the necessary high precision, and because its subtle glow goes well with the high silk contents of the knitting yarns.

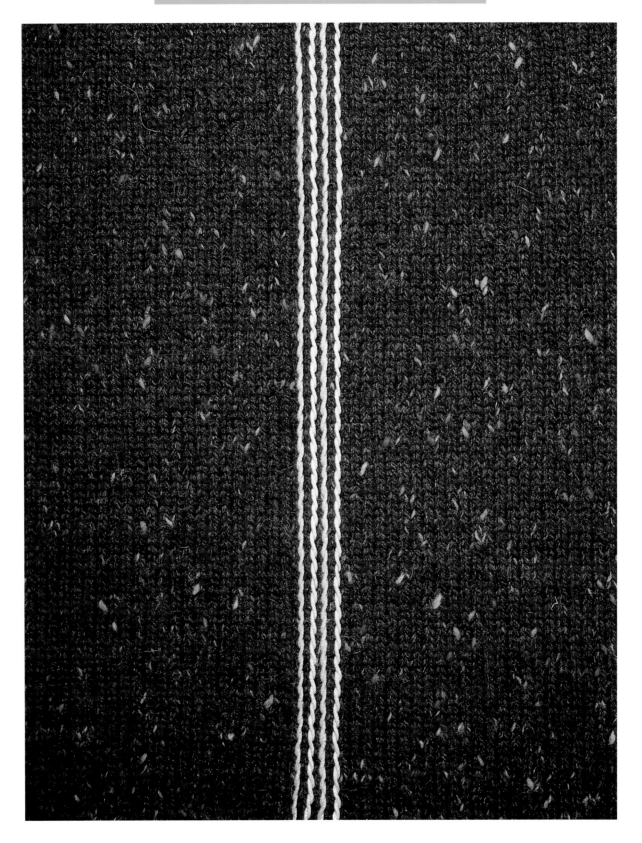

SAMPLE 44

● ● ●KNITTING● ● ●

Stocking stitch with purl line along vertical ladder-stitch seam, in yarn 19.

● ● ●EMBROIDERY● ● ●

Satin stitch in yarn 32 (two strands).

A purl stitch was worked two stitches away from the edge to be sewn so that the satin stitch could be worked easily along a couple of clear lines and would not become crooked. The ladder stitch took in one of the stitches from each side, leaving two knit stitches between the purl-stitch lines. To purl the three edge stitches instead was also considered, but soon dismissed. The seam area would have sunk, drawing the two knit sides together – just as if it had been part of a rib.

The navy of the furry mohair needed a light contrast, such as the gently glossy yellow of the silk. This was used double to fill the large mohair stitches. The two strands were kept parallel, and the resulting line is very straight and even.

The seam inside the satin stitch works rather like padding. To make the seam even more raised and rounded, the embroidery was worked slightly tighter than usual.

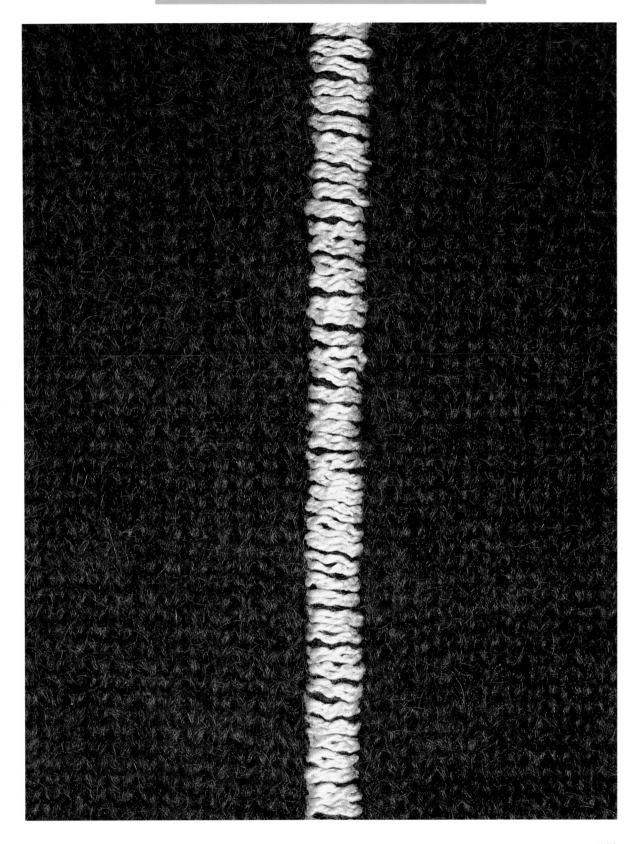

SAMPLE 45

● ● ● KNITTING ● ● ●

Reverse stocking stitch with knit band along vertical ladder-stitch seam in yarn 23.

● ● ● EMBROIDERY ● ● ●

Double line of cross stitch in yarn 22.

This sample was knitted with the purl side showing for the reasons given for sample 16. The three edge stitches, however, were knitted. This provided good edges for the embroidery and also made it stand out from the rest. After the seam was sewn, a panel of four knit stitches resulted.

Some embroidery yarns are chosen for contrast, and some because they blend in. On this occasion, angora was chosen for its blending qualities: its characteristic furriness goes very well with that of the knitting yarn. Mohair, even of exactly the same shade, would have been far less successful.

There are two rows of cross stitch. The first one is four knitted rows wide, and is worked just outside the knit band. The second row keeps down the long arms of the first one, while creating a more interesting pattern. It is worked along the same knitted rows picked up in the first row, but between the first and second knit stitches at either side of the seam line.

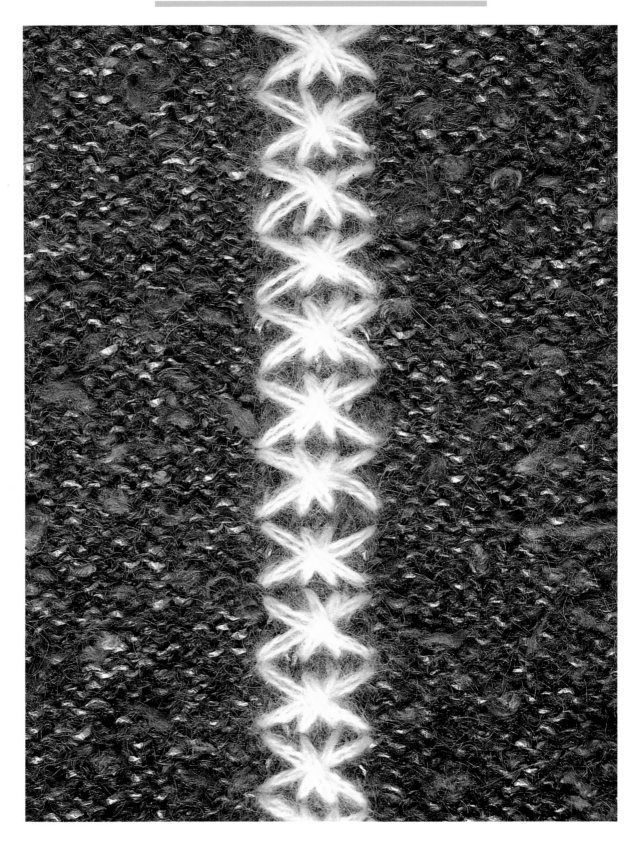

SAMPLE 46

● ● ●KNITTING● ● ●
Stocking stitch with ladder-stitch raglan seam, in yarn 36.

● ● ●EMBROIDERY● ● ●
Four-sided stitch in yarns 33 and 39.

The decreases for this sample were worked four stitches away from the edge, following the slant of the seam. Knit-two-together decreases were used to the right of the seam. Slip-slip-knit decreases (as explained on page 73) were used to the left.

After the seam was sewn, a band of six knitted stitches could be seen to run across the sample. Two lines of elongated four-sided stitches were worked over this band.

The long sides of the four-sided stitches span five knitted rows. The short sides span three stitches. Work into the centre of those stitches at the edge of the band, and just past the seam line.

The second embroidery row is worked on the other side of the seam, so that it overlaps the first row. The rectangles made by the two rows are offset, so that the short sides don't clash.

To complement the deep blue of the knitting cotton, two contrasting yellow yarns were chosen. One is a strong canary yellow, smooth and ribbon-like. The other is an acid yellow, rough and unplied. The first one is cotton; the second one linen.

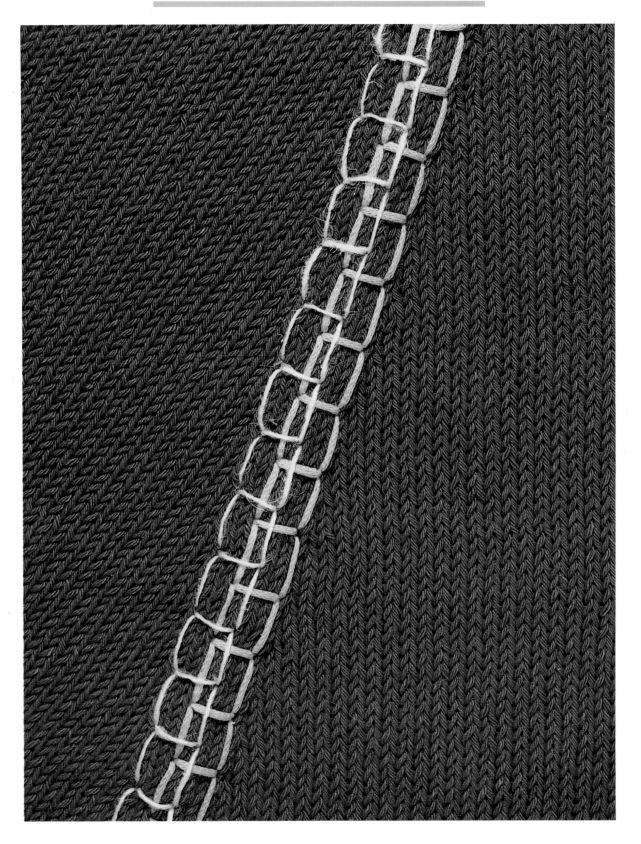

SAMPLE 47

● ● ●KNITTING● ● ●

Stocking stitch with ladder-stitch raglan seam in yarn 11.

● ● ●EMBROIDERY● ● ●

Zigzag backstitch in yarn 10.

The decreases for this raglan slant in the opposite way to the seam, so that no band like that of sample 46 appears. Instead, you get visible, isolated decreases. Use slip-slip-knit (see page 73) to the right of the seam and knit-two-together to its left.

Alternately, the stitches worked together for a decrease were the fifth and sixth from the edge, and the second and third. This gave two sets of reference points on which to base the first row of zigzag backstitch.

Once the seam was sewn, five shades of plain lopi wool were selected to embroider the speckled, knitted lopi.

If you look at the colours carefully, you will see that the seemingly complex pattern is built quite easily. The two rows of soft brick, one at either side, come first. They are worked into the decreases at either side of the seam. All the other rows are parallel to these two. Second come the two rows of primrose yellow, one stitch inside the first two. These two rows meet on the seam line. Third come two rows in maize, again one stitch inside the previous pair. They cross each other, and they meet the soft-brick row from the opposite side. Finally, come the two sage-green rows, crossing each other straight away, and all the colours from the other side later.

SAMPLE 48

●●●KNITTING●●●
Stocking stitch with horizontal knitted seam in yarn 4 (double knitting).

●●●EMBROIDERY●●●
Backstitch also in yarn 4 (tapestry wool).

The two sides of this sample were not sewn, but cast off together. Put the two pieces of knitting against each other, with the two wrong sides showing. With a third knitting needle, work one stitch from the front piece together with one stitch from the back piece. Cast off in the usual way, as you progress along the row.

The arrow pattern was preset on the knitting. Six rows short of the top, a k6, p1 sequence was established. This was made to travel one stitch to the left on the piece below the seam, and one stitch to the right on the piece above it.

Four shades of tapestry wool were then used to follow both sides of the purl lines, and both sides of the seam line, with backstitch – matching one embroidery stitch to one knitting stitch. Sunny yellow and egg-yolk yellow follow the seam, and branch into the arrows. Soft olive green and deep copper outline the remaining side of the arrows.

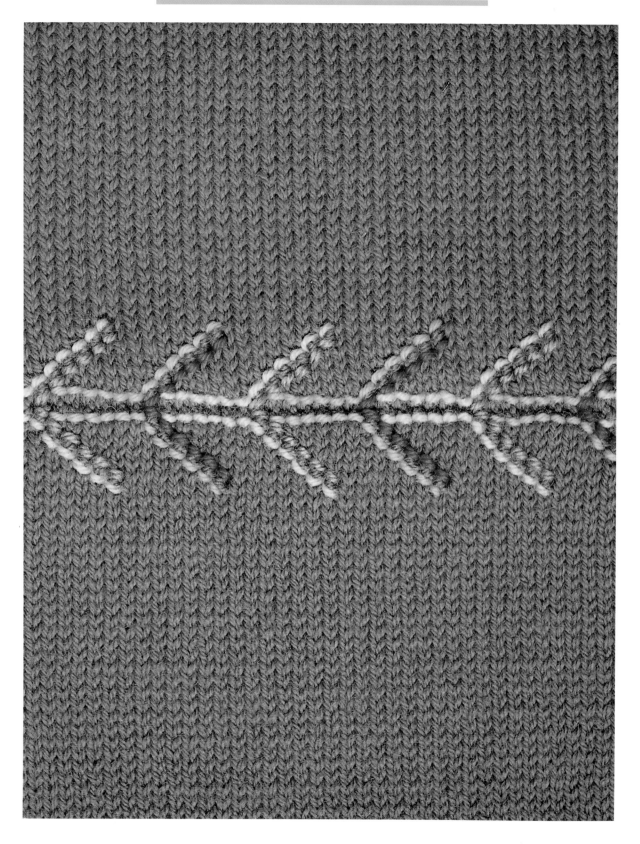

SUPPLIERS

YARNS

The yarns used in this book have been supplied by the manufacturers that follow.

Do remember to enclose a stamped addressed envelope when enquiring about shades, prices or stockists in your area.

Alafoss of Iceland
Lopi wool and other classic yarns

British distributor:
Scotnord Yarns Ltd
Chase Mill
Winchester Road
Bishop's Waltham
Hampshire
SO3 1AH

Mail-order retail:
Scotnord Yarns Ltd
P.O. Box 27
Athey Street
Macclesfield
Cheshire
SK11 8

American distributor:
Reynolds Yarns Inc.
15 Oser Avenue
Hauppauge
New York 11788

Avocet Hand Knitting Yarns
High fashion yarns

Hammerain House
Hookstone Avenue
Harrogate
Yorkshire
HG2 8ER

Mail-order retail:
Bedford Woolshop
The Old Arcade
Bedford
MK40 1NS

Colinette Yarns
Special dyes on natural fibres

Wholesale and mail-order retail:
Cadmium Studio
Park Lane House
High Street
Welshpool
Powys
Wales

Colourtwist
10 Mayfield Avenue Industrial Park
Weyhill
Andover
Hampshire
SP11 8HU

D.M.C.
Tapestry wools and embroidery cottons

British distributor:
Dunlicraft Ltd
Pullman Road
Wigston
Leicester
LE8 2DY

Mail-order retail:
The Royal School of Needlework
5 King Street
London
WC2 8HN

American distributor:
The DMC Corporation
107 Trumbull Street
Elizabeth
New Jersey 07206

Jamieson & Smith
Shetland wool

Wholesale and mail-order retail:
90 North Road
Lerwick
Shetland Isles
ZE1 0PQ

American mail order:
Tomato Factory Yarn Co.
8 Church Street
Lambertville
New Jersey 08530

Lodge Enterprises
Short runs of special twists
in natural fibres

Mail-order retail:
56A Ayres Street
London
SE1 1EU

Rowan Yarns
Classic yarns in natural fibres

British distributor
Green Lane Mill
Holmfirth
West Yorkshire

Mail-order retail:
Ries Wools
242 High Holborn
London
WC1V 7DZ

American distributor:
Westminster Trading
Corporation
5 Northern Boulevard
Amherst
New Hampshire 03031

Tiber Yarns
High fashion yarns

British distributor:
Laines Couture
Osney Mead
Oxford
OX2 0ER

Mail-order retail:
Honee Bee
7 Gosport Street
Lymington
Hampshire
SO41 9BG

American distributor:
Merino Wool Company Inc
16 West 19th Street
New York 10011

20th Century Yarns
Special dyes on natural fibres

Mail-order retail:
The Red House
Guilsborough
Northants
NN6 8PU

GRIDS

Rectangular Chartwell True Knit grids in different ratios for the accurate charting of knitting are manufactured by:

H.W. Peel and Co. Ltd
Norwester House
Fairway Drive
Greenford
Middlesex
UB6 8PW

Main British distributor:
D.K.M.S.
c/o AA Distribution Services Ltd
Dunhams Lane
Letchworth
Hertfordshire
SG6 1LS

Mail-order retail:
The Textile Bookshop
Tynwald Mills
St John's
Isle of Man

and

Fibercrafts
Style Cottage
Lower Eashing
Godalming
Surrey
GU7 2QD

These grids are not available in America at the time of writing. Rectangular grids in two sizes, but very similar ratios, can be obtained from:

Schoolhouse Press
6899 Cary Bluff
Pittsville
Wisconsin 54466

PATTERNS

Montse Stanley has designed a collection of patterns for embroidered sweaters, exclusively for Jaeger. A list of yarn stockists is available from:

Jaeger Handknitting Limited
McMullen Road
Darlington
Co. Durham
DL1 1YH

In America:
Jaeger Handknitting Yarns
212 Middlesex Avenue
Chester
Connecticut 06412

INDEX